The Knights Hospitaller

A Captivating Guide to a Medieval and Early Modern Catholic Military Order and Their Impact on the Crusades, the Great Siege of Malta, and the Middle Ages

© Copyright 2023 - All rights reserved.

The content contained within this book may not be reproduced, duplicated, or transmitted without direct written permission from the author or the publisher.

Under no circumstances will any blame or legal responsibility be held against the publisher, or author, for any damages, reparation, or monetary loss due to the information contained within this book, either directly or indirectly.

Legal Notice:

This book is copyright protected. It is only for personal use. You cannot amend, distribute, sell, use, quote, or paraphrase any part, or the content within this book, without the consent of the author or publisher.

Disclaimer Notice:

Please note the information contained within this document is for educational and entertainment purposes only. All effort has been executed to present accurate, up-to-date, reliable, and complete information. No warranties of any kind are declared or implied. Readers acknowledge that the author is not engaging in the rendering of legal, financial, medical, or professional advice. The content within this book has been derived from various sources. Please consult a licensed professional before attempting any techniques outlined in this book.

By reading this document, the reader agrees that under no circumstances is the author responsible for any losses, direct or indirect, that are incurred as a result of the use of the information contained within this document, including, but not limited to, errors, omissions, or inaccuracies.

Free Bonus from Captivating History (Available for a Limited time)

Hi History Lovers!

Now you have a chance to join our exclusive history list so you can get your first history ebook for free as well as discounts and a potential to get more history books for free! Simply visit the link below to join.

Captivatinghistory.com/ebook

Also, make sure to follow us on Facebook, Twitter and Youtube by searching for Captivating History.

Table of Contents

INTRODUCTION 1
CHAPTER ONE – ORIGINS OF THE ORDER 5
CHAPTER TWO – FROM THE HOSPITAL TO THE BATTLEFIELD 15
CHAPTER THREE – HIGH HIGHS AND LOW LOWS 29
CHAPTER FOUR – DARKEST HOUR 44
CHAPTER FIVE – ABANDONING THE HOLY LAND 57
CHAPTER SIX – HOSPITALLER RHODES 68
CHAPTER SEVEN – HOSPITALLER MALTA 84
CONCLUSION 90
HERE'S ANOTHER BOOK BY CAPTIVATING HISTORY THAT YOU MIGHT LIKE 93
FREE BONUS FROM CAPTIVATING HISTORY (AVAILABLE FOR A LIMITED TIME) 94
SOURCES 95

Introduction

The history of Christianity spans over two millennia and is rich with an array of amazing details and narratives that are not solely embedded in the religion's doctrines or holy scriptures. The Christian world has witnessed many developments throughout the centuries that have greatly affected the overall course of history and have shaped the lives of countless people. Out of all those developments, it comes as no surprise that the Crusades are considered to have been a pivotal point. The era of the Crusades was a period when an ambitious and already mature Christendom first tried to assert its position of dominance in an ever-changing world with new threats that could potentially undermine it. For two hundred years, the crusaders struggled for control of the Holy Land against the rivaling powers of the Muslim world, producing one of the most iconic but, at the same time, bloodiest periods of medieval times. Certainly, the legacy of the Crusades is vast. One of its various consequences continued to directly impact the medieval world order for many years, even after the end of the last crusader kingdoms in Outremer: the establishment of religious military orders, namely the Knights Templar and the Knights Hospitaller. The Knights Hospitaller is officially known as the Order of Knights of the Hospital of Saint John of Jerusalem.

Examining the existence of these unique institutions is compelling for curious individuals who wish to understand the much larger history of medieval Christianity, which is rooted in conflict, schisms, faith, and the pursuit of power. However, out of the two orders mentioned above, as well as the Teutonic Order, which would be created somewhat later but still became an iconic part of European history, the Knights Hospitaller arguably attracts the least attention from the general public and scholars. It is really an interesting phenomenon that the Hospitallers get less love than their Templar or Teutonic counterparts, despite the fact they have the earliest origins and still continue to exist in different shapes and forms today. While they deeply affected the course of the Christian world, both in the Holy Land and in Europe for many centuries, a feeling may arise that the Hospitallers are sometimes overshadowed by the Templars, who are represented more in popular culture due to their infamous history and mysterious elements. The Hospitallers are even overshadowed by the Teutons, who were more powerful and more directly involved in medieval Europe.

This book will tell the history of the Knights Hospitaller, an iconic Catholic military order from the Holy Land that slowly transformed from a small hospital dedicated to treating the Christian pilgrims in Jerusalem to one of the most professional and feared military institutions of the time. The history of the Knights Hospitaller is rooted in its humble and noble origins, and the order's path to power and greatness is certainly very intriguing. As already mentioned, the Hospitallers would never grow to be as rich or influential as the Templars or would never come to directly control the amount of territory as the Teutons. Nevertheless, at the height of their power, the Hospitaller knights were respected throughout the Christian and Muslim worlds. They continued to play an active, independent role after the defeat of the crusaders, although they were forced to leave the Holy Land. Still, they never stopped dreaming of returning to their glory days.

There is much less controversy when it comes to the Hospitallers than there is with the Templars, who were infamously run down and prosecuted, charged with abandoning the very thing that made them famously respected in the first place: their astuteness and dedication for the Christian cause. On the contrary, the Hospitallers were perhaps the noblest of the orders, continuing to serve their purpose even during the toughest of times and fighting the enemies of the Christian world to the bitter end.

The first part of the book will be concerned with the origins of the order, which actually goes back a couple of hundred years before the Crusades. The Order of the Knights Hospitaller would develop and flourish after the arrival of the crusaders in Jerusalem in 1099. And it would only be after the establishment of the Crusader States that the order would adopt its military role. Before that, the Knights Hospitaller had operated a hospital for Christian pilgrims in Jerusalem since the 7th century. The hospital had been commissioned to be built by Pope Gregory I in 603. For many years, even before the thought of the Crusades and reclaiming the Holy Land seriously entered the minds of the Europeans, the Hospitallers, although they did not yet have that name, struggled under the control of different Muslim leaders. Yet they maintained their hospital and treated the pilgrims, thanks to help from their European donors.

The middle chapters of the book will cover the crusader era and the subsequent development of the Knights Hospitaller into a powerful military order. We shall look at the causes and consequences of the later Crusades and try to understand the role of the Hospitallers in those campaigns. Throughout these years, the Hospitallers, just like the Templars, would be assigned control of different castles in Outremer, which would grow their direct influence and their status among their enemies. The Hospitallers served as stalwart defenders of the faith and became one of the most feared warriors in the Levant. These chapters will also examine the political processes that came to shape the course of Hospitaller history, leading to the eventual defeat of the crusaders by the end of the 13th century and the subsequent exile of the Hospitallers to Cyprus and then to the island of Rhodes, where they would be headquartered for the years to come until a new challenge would be presented to them.

The final chapters of the book will talk about the struggles of the exiled order when they were confronted with a weakened Byzantine Empire and a growing hostile Ottoman Empire. We will look at the several battles against the Ottomans in which the Knights Hospitaller participated, including at Smyrna, Rhodes, and Malta. After leaving the Holy Land, the order would try to regain much of its influence, coming into the possession of different Mediterranean islands and castles, but they would never quite manage to withstand the full might of their foes without the cohesive support of the Christian world, which would be just as divided as ever. In the end, we will examine the legacy of the Knights Hospitaller, which still persists today in very interesting forms.

Chapter One – Origins of the Order

Christendom in Crisis

In the Early Middle Ages, after the fall of the Western Roman Empire, Europe was a very different place from what it would be about a thousand years later after the fall of Constantinople in 1453. Still, as the political geography of the region transformed throughout the centuries of war and bloodshed, one important thing that remained was the role and status of Christianity in the different European states. Western and much of central Europe were already deeply Christian before the 7th century CE when Prophet Muhammad first started preaching Islam to the Arabs. To modern-day readers who are used to their secular lives, where religion is largely separated from everyday activities, it is perhaps almost impossible to fully grasp the sheer presence of Christianity in the lives of early medieval Europeans. Living a good life meant living a religious life and upholding the principles from the Bible and the Gospels, especially for those born in higher-class families.

Still, although all of those who knew how to read and write in Europe tried their best to live religious lives, donating to the church and studying religious texts, the majority of them never had the chance to visit the place where it all had originated: the holy city of Jerusalem. For them, Jerusalem was a legendary place. They had read about its marvelous nature and realized its importance in the development and growth of the Christian religion. Many also knew the city had been a constant target for non-Christians for many years, with the Byzantine Empire—a bulwark of Christianity in the East—constantly trying to maintain its control over Jerusalem. During the height of the Byzantine Empire's power in the 4th century, Emperor Constantine the Great managed to fend off the empire's enemies and devoted great resources toward the reconstruction of many of Jerusalem's holy sites, including the Church of the Holy Sepulchre, which housed the True Cross (the cross upon which Jesus had been crucified). Byzantine control, which would last until the 7th century, meant that European pilgrims who were devoted to their faith and ready to leave behind their lives traveled to the Holy City in waves, trying to see the marvels of Jerusalem themselves.

However, starting from the 7th century, the pressure exerted upon Byzantium by its enemies eventually resulted in the loss of Jerusalem for Christendom. Sassanid Shah Khosrow II, the ruler of Persia, took the city in 614 from the Byzantines, imprisoning and executing many of its inhabitants, damaging religious sites, and even taking a part of the True Cross as a trophy for himself. Although the Byzantines would be able to briefly regain control of the city and the relic under Emperor Heraclius in 630, they would once again lose it eight years later, this time to Caliph Umar ibn-al Khattab. Thus, beginning in 638, the Muslim Arabs would slowly start the Islamification of Jerusalem. And as Islam spread throughout the Middle East, North Africa, and Iberia, by the end of the 8th century, the Holy City was firmly under different Muslim rulers' control.

Still, the flow of Christian pilgrims from Europe to Jerusalem continued, although this time, the pilgrims had a difficult time safely getting to their destination, as they were subjected to constant harassment from the Muslims. Many of them would outright perish even before they got to the Holy City. Those who were lucky enough to reach Jerusalem and get back to their homes in Europe would usually bring terrible news of Christians being slaughtered by the heathen Muslims and the relentless attacks they would suffer throughout their time in the Levant. Thus, by the time the Europeans decided to act in the name of God and launch the First Crusade to regain control of the Holy Land, the news of the horrible mistreatment of Christian pilgrims was nothing new. The fact that thousands of devout Europeans continued to travel to Jerusalem proved they were ready to face the challenges that awaited them just to get to their destination. There was another reason for launching such an ambitious military campaign against the Muslims, one rooted not in religion but in politics.

The talk of the First Crusade really began in Europe after the arrival of a new formidable threat from Asia, which was able to crush the Byzantine Empire in a decisive battle in the late 11th century. The Seljuk Turks, nomadic warrior peoples from central Asia, started migrating from their homeland to the West, relentlessly fighting their way through Persia and eventually reaching the Byzantine lands and the Levant, much of which was controlled by the Egyptian Fatimid Caliphate at that time. By this time, the Seljuks had converted to Sunni Islam and were fighting the *ghazwa*—a holy war in the name of Prophet Muhammad to spread their religion. They crushed their enemies, including the Byzantines in the Battle of Manzikert in 1071, and even continued their advance to the Fatimids, who were Shi'a Muslims, therefore making them their enemies.

Two years after Manzikert, the Seljuks captured Jerusalem from the Fatimids, sacking the city and massacring its inhabitants, including thousands of Shi'a Muslims. The Seljuks' domination and the subsequent weakening of the Byzantine Empire, which had been greatly reduced in size throughout its struggles with the Muslims, rang the alarm for the Europeans to take up arms and launch the First Crusade to reclaim Jerusalem.

Crucially, in 1095, Pope Urban II received Byzantine diplomats who had been sent by Emperor Alexios I Komnenos. The diplomats brought grave news of the Seljuk rampage in Anatolia and the Levant. They urged the pope to organize the Christian nations to send help to relieve the pressure on the Byzantine Empire, which stood as the last defense between the Muslims and Christian Europe. It has to be noted that the Great Schism had already happened by this time, with the Orthodox Byzantines having split off from the Western Catholics due to differences in the interpretation of the holy scriptures and the ambition to become independent from papal rule. So, for Alexios to approach the pope in such turbulent times and ask for help meant the situation was truly desperate (although the Byzantine legation did, no doubt, overexaggerate the threat of the Seljuks). Still, after thinking over the matter, Pope Urban II believed in the noble mission of reclaiming the Holy Land and perhaps hoped to get political favors in case of a successful expedition. The pope called for a council to assemble in Clermont, which would change the course of history forever.

In November of 1095, during the Council of Clermont, Pope Urban II addressed the hundreds of clergy and nobles who had assembled and urged them to launch a military campaign to reclaim the Holy Land from the Muslims. In his famous speech, he described the atrocities of Christendom's enemies and promised eternal salvation and glory to everyone who was brave enough to join the holy cause. Instantly, the cries of "Deus vult!" ("God wills it!") echoed throughout Clermont. The assembled nobles fell to their knees, swearing they would fulfill the pope's request to reclaim Jerusalem and bring justice to the Christian world. After about a year and a half of preparations, during which time the pope traveled from city to city, trying to convince as many people as possible to join the expedition, the First Crusade would be launched.

Fully covering the First Crusade or, for that matter, any of the Crusades is well beyond the scope of this book. Still, we should mention that it took three years for the Christians to accomplish their goal—three years filled with desertion, attrition, illness, bloodshed, and a whole array of problems. Finally, after tirelessly marching through Anatolia and being confronted by the Muslims nearly every step of the way, and after overcoming the logistical difficulties that were innate with an expedition of such magnitude, the crusaders finally captured Jerusalem in July of 1099 after a forty-day siege. Led by Godfrey of Bouillon, one of the four commanders of the First Crusade, tens of thousands of Frankish knights charged into the streets of the Holy City, massacring the Fatimid garrison down to the last man (the Fatimid Caliphate had regained control of the city in 1093 from the Seljuks, but the crusaders had fought the latter on their way). They were also relentless to all other non-Christian inhabitants of the city, butchering thousands of Muslims and Jews, who constituted the majority of the city's population, as they ironically cried out, "Deus vult!"

The First Crusade would come to an end with the capture of Jerusalem. The crusaders established four Latin kingdoms in the lands they wrestled away from the Muslims on the Mediterranean coast of the Levant: the Kingdom of Jerusalem, with Godfrey of Bouillon as the first king; the Principality of Antioch under Bohemond I of Taranto; the County of Edessa under Baldwin of Boulogne, who would also become king of Jerusalem after Godfrey's sudden passing in 1100; and the County of Tripoli, which would be headed by Raymond IV of Toulouse. As the crusaders began to rule the conquered lands and keep the Muslims away, they would soon come to realize they had a very difficult task at hand.

Origins of the Hospital

About twenty years after the conquest of Outremer, the Knights Hospitaller and the Knights Templar would become the two main religious military orders, taking up arms to aid the Latins in defending the pilgrims on their way to the Holy Land. The Templar Order would be established following the events of the First Crusade with the purpose of defending the pilgrims. However, the origins of the Hospitaller Order go way back, even before the conception of the Crusades or of any talk of reclaiming the Holy City.

In fact, there had long been a Christian hospital in Jerusalem to treat the Christian pilgrims that arrived in the city. The first had been commissioned to be built by Pope Gregory I in 603, not even a decade after the city had been captured by the Persians. As we mentioned above, the pilgrims continued to journey to Jerusalem, and since the city was now held by non-Christians, it made sense for a Christian hospital to be set up, one funded by the papacy. Thus, the hospital started its existence in the 7th century and was running even when the city changed hands a couple of times between the Byzantines and Arabs in the following years, surviving off donations from Europe. However, at the turn of the 11th century, around the year 1005, when Fatimid Caliph al-Hakim captured the city, he ordered the hospital, along with much of the rest of the Christian sites, to be destroyed due to his personal dislike of Christians.

We know from the accounts of William of Tyre, a chronicler whose records give us the understanding of the Holy Land in the age of the Crusades, that the Italian Christians from Amalfi would contribute to the rebuilding of the hospital sometime in the 11th century, although the exact date is unknown. The Italians had long engaged in trade with the Fatimids and supposedly acquired a right to build a Christian hospital to treat the pilgrims in the city. A merchant from Amalfi by the name of Mauro of Pantaleone is thought to have mainly funded the construction of the hospital, which was visited by Archbishop Giovanni of Amalfi during his pilgrimage to Jerusalem in the 1070s. It has been revealed that the archbishop was greeted by the Italians who resided in the city and operated two hospices, one for men, dedicated to St. John the Baptist, and one for women, dedicated to St. Mary Magdalene, in the Muristan district of the city. By this time, the control of the city had been assumed by the Seljuks, but despite the horrific accounts presented by the Byzantine legation to Pope Urban II, it seems they were far more tolerant toward the Christians. Perhaps the Seljuks would have rather had a Latin Catholic hospice in Jerusalem than tolerate a Greek Orthodox institution for the Christians of the city since the Byzantines were their enemies.

At the time of the Fatimid reconquest of Jerusalem in 1093, just before the launch of the First Crusade, it seems the hospice was headed by a man named Gerard, a devout Italian abbot who would be referred to as Blessed Gerard by his contemporaries. It appears that Gerard was a respected man since he and the rest of the monks who worked in the hospices were not exiled from Jerusalem, unlike many other Christians who were forced to leave the city before the First Crusade arrived. The Fatimids implemented this measure to avoid an insurgence during the siege. Gerard greeted the crusaders when they brutally entered the city in July of 1099. Unlike the crusaders, who relentlessly exiled, imprisoned, and killed all non-Catholics of the city (including the Orthodox Christians), Gerard and his men tended to all the ill and wounded. They admitted all of the needy, despite their religion, to their hospices.

The point where Blessed Gerard and his men officially become the Knights Hospitaller is unclear. It seems that it was a gradual process that took place over the span of two decades after the capture of Jerusalem. What we do know is that both Godfrey of Bouillon and Baldwin I made contact with Gerard and the Christian hospices, which certainly helped the hospices increase their reputation. As the Latin kingdoms started to firmly establish their position in Outremer, the flow of pilgrims to the Holy Land renewed once again, with the Italian merchants transporting those devout Catholics who wanted to travel and see the marvels of Jerusalem. The ports of Tyre and Jaffa were crucial, as they were located relatively close to the Holy City and were used by the Italians to drop off the pilgrims, who would then head to Jerusalem.

However, as the months passed after the crusaders' success, it soon became clear that defending their newly gained lands posed a great challenge to the Latins. There were several reasons for this. The first and most obvious is the fact that the Latin kingdoms were surrounded by hostile Muslims, who had far better knowledge and adaptability to the region than the Europeans. Raids on small towns, ports, trade caravans, and, most of all, pilgrims were very common in the early days after the end of the First Crusade. Small bands of Muslim raiders, who either operated independently or were issued commands from the Fatimids, would relentlessly harass those who left the safety of the city walls with mounted archers. These kinds of attacks made it almost impossible for the typically heavy-armored crusaders to strike back effectively.

Another reason behind the troubles of the Latins was the simple lack of manpower. After the First Crusade, most of the knights who had taken part in the journey and had become seasoned veterans in the process had left for home, where they were greeted as heroes and legends. The First Crusade's leaders did stay behind to set up new Catholic lands in Outremer. While some of the crusaders had embarked on the expedition to attain holy salvation and see the birthplace of Christianity for themselves, for a large portion of the warriors, triumph in the campaign meant a lot of riches and booty, not to speak of the glorious songs and poems they expected to be composed about them back home in Europe. Thus, after a large part of the crusaders decided to head home after taking Jerusalem, the Latin rulers in Outremer were confronted with a serious lack of capable soldiers who could fight to defend the Holy Land from the Muslims. It was very difficult to replenish the numbers after the Christian men were slain in battles. The pilgrims needed the most protection, as the journey from Jaffa to Jerusalem was not safe at all, and a permanent military presence was required for a safe passage, something that was really difficult to afford.

The Knights of Saint John

During this time, the hospital was being run by Blessed Gerard and had even managed to increase its reputation among the new rulers of Jerusalem, who donated a lot of resources like funds and horses to keep it running. Donations also came from Europe and locals, who saw it as a noble thing to give to such an institution. This increase in reputation also resulted in the hospital of St. John, which was headed by Gerard, separating from the hospital of St. Mary, its twin institution. This separation was confirmed in 1113 by an official papal bull issued by Pope Paschal II named *Pie postulatio voluntatis*. The bull officially confirmed the Hospital of St. John as a separate religious order, a declaration that would be later reaffirmed by the other popes. All in all, by the mid-1110s, it seems that Gerard and company had achieved enough success to operate as a separate institution, combining the roles of caretaking in their hospice and of monks in the associated churches into the order. This resulted in more volunteers joining the order.

Sometime during the twenty-year period after the capture of Jerusalem, the Hospitallers, although they were not yet being called that, started assuming a military role. We have already mentioned that hostilities between the Christians and the Muslims never truly ceased throughout this time, and Baldwin I desperately needed men to rule his realm securely. Thus, it seems that the adoption of a quasi-military role immediately after the capture of Jerusalem came as a natural, practical thing for the Hospitallers, who are even mentioned to have accompanied King Baldwin I on his expedition to take Jaffa as early as 1102. Around this time, the members of the hospital begin to be referred to as the "soldiers of Christ," which alludes to the fact that they had already started participating in military activities. Being dedicated to the care and well-being of the pilgrims and having received gracious donations, which also included weapons and horses, the responsibilities of the Hospitallers slowly started to include accompanying and defending the pilgrims on their journey, not only offering them the services of a hospital once they arrived in Jerusalem.

The monastic Order of St. John continued its existence as an independent institution, having obtained this right from the pope. It also became increasingly militaristic throughout the 1110s. However, it would be Gerard's successor, Raymond du Puy, who would push for a more clearly active military role for the order after taking over as the grand master in 1123. Gerard, the first leader of the order, passed away sometime around 1118 or 1119. Before the election of Raymond du Puy, it appears there was an interim period where the order was headed by two individuals: Pierre de Barcelone and Boyant Roger. However, nothing is really known about them except for the fact they were two brothers of the order. Raymond, a French knight who probably took part in the First Crusade and then joined the hospital after the Christians' victory, is sometimes referred to as the first true grand master of the Knights Hospitaller since the title was never used during Gerard's time. During Raymond's long tenure, the order's militarization exponentially increased its popularity in the Christian world.

The Hospitallers started combining the military aspect of defending the pilgrims on their journey to Jerusalem with their core role of caretaking and living a chaste monkish lifestyle. The second half of the 1110s also saw the creation of a similar order, which was also located in Jerusalem and based around the Temple Mount. A band of nine devout knights, led by Hugh de Payens and Geoffrey de Saint-Omer, assembled before the new King Baldwin II in 1118, offering to create a military institution that would not only dedicate its life to the protection of pilgrims but also to all of Outremer. The generous Baldwin II granted them a permanent residence at the ruins of the Temple of Solomon and accepted their request, providing them with resources and weapons to rebuild the Temple. Thus, the Knights Templar was born just a few years after the Hospitallers had greatly increased their presence and reputation among the Latins.

Although the Hospitaller and the Templar orders were completely separate institutions (they were independent of each other and the king's jurisdiction; the latter would obtain this privilege officially from the pope later on), there were quite a few similarities between the two. Still, the Hospitallers and the Templars specialized in different aspects. The Templars took vows of chastity, obedience, and poverty, but they were, first and foremost, a military institution. They were warrior monks, dedicated to the fight for Christendom against the heathens and ready to do whatever that role might involve. They wore white tunics with a red cross, which symbolized their martyrdom and readiness to die in battle for God, which was seen as the greatest honor of all. In contrast, the Hospitallers wore black clothing with a white cross, emphasizing that they cared less about themselves and more about the hospital's charitable work, although they were just as fierce as the Templars.

For the next few hundred years, the Templars and the Hospitallers grew to be two of the most famous and powerful Catholic military orders in the world. However, their general approach to their duties and roles was drastically different from the very beginning. For example, while the Templar grand masters embarked on a European journey soon after being acknowledged by Baldwin II in Jerusalem to recruit volunteers and gain funding from the devout Catholics who wanted to donate to a holy cause, the Hospitallers were far more modest, sticking to their humble origins and residing mainly in their quarter near the Holy Sepulchre. They slowly grew their hospital to include about one thousand beds, giving care not only to the pilgrims but also to the city's inhabitants. Hospitaller doctors were employed at all times, giving much-needed care to the poor. They often used new medical methods to treat their patients. The Hospitallers lived mainly by the principles of Saint Augustine, placing great emphasis on one's personal responsibility to attain salvation, which for them meant providing care to the needy.

On the other hand, the Templars were influenced by Bernard of Clairvaux of the Cistercian monastic order, which was rather popular at the time. The order underlined the moral values of austerity and living simple lives. Still, both orders fundamentally believed that dying while fighting for the glory of God was the highest honor of them all. And this attitude contributed to the development of a new kind of knighthood in medieval Europe: a knighthood that placed emphasis on piety and bravery.

Chapter Two – From the Hospital to the Battlefield

The Order Grows

The Hospitallers had already gained quite a bit of notoriety from accompanying King Baldwin I on several of his military campaigns throughout the 1110s before the election of Raymond du Puy as their grand master. The order would start to grow exponentially after 1123. New knights came from Europe to join the order, and new material possessions were entrusted to the Hospitallers throughout the 1120s and the 1130s. In this regard, the Hospitallers appear to have been quite similar to their Templar counterparts, only, as mentioned above, Templar Grand Master Hugues de Payens actually visited Europe to obtain donations from the nobles and the order's status via an official order from the pope.

As word spread around Europe of military orders being formed in Outremer that not only accepted but asked for volunteers from Europe, thousands decided that it was the right thing to do. The thing that attracted the young men of Europe to the Templars and the Hospitallers was the tempting idea of becoming a warrior in the name of Christ. However, being a good warrior was only one part of being a Templar or Hospitaller. The more important aspects of the two orders were following the principles and ethics of the brotherhood, which were quite hard for the average European man at the time. The orders placed great emphasis on chastity, poverty, and piety, and they did not always accept those who wished to become knights. Any new recruit had to undergo a couple of years of training and live with the brothers of the orders before they could become full-fledged members.

Many were drawn to Outremer in search of glory, especially the younger sons of richer noble families of Europe who were in line to inherit nothing from their fathers. While the older sons trained to become knights in their own respect, the younger sons were free to pursue whatever they wanted. And due to the reputation of the orders, joining one of them seemed as noble of a deed as staying home. This was also because the line between good and evil was clearly drawn in Outremer, as the pious and righteous Christians were fighting the heathen Muslims. Due to the political drama in Europe during the 11th and 12th centuries, which involved complicated tensions like the situation between the pope and the Holy Roman Empire or the constant wars among the Catholic nations, it was not always clear what the best option was for aspiring knights.

As the years passed, the Hospitallers started to play a bigger role in the military activities of Outremer. Due to Raymond du Puy's connections in France and the subsequent growth of the Hospitallers in Iberia, where the Reconquista against the Muslims was well underway, the number of Hospitallers appears to have been around five hundred, not counting all the squires and other personnel the grand master needed to run the order's possessions. These five hundred or so knights, along with their Templar counterparts, were the most professional forces in Outremer and Europe. They often offered their help to the sovereigns of the Latin kingdoms against the Muslims. They never chose to fight against other Christians, even if the Latins descended into conflict with each other.

The order's possessions also grew drastically during this period, as the Hospitallers were granted different fortifications throughout the Holy Land. The crusaders acknowledged the strength and discipline of the military orders, and they were more than happy to give them control of several castles in the dangerous lands that bordered the Muslim dominions. The first of the castles donated to the Hospitallers in Outremer was the one in Qalansawe in 1128 on the coast north of the city of Arsuf. In 1136, King Fulk of Jerusalem granted the Hospitallers control of Bayt Jibrin in Israel, around which the order would soon develop a village with Frankish dwellers.

Perhaps the most iconic Hospitaller possession was the mighty castle of Krak des Chevaliers, which at that time was in the territory of the County of Tripoli. Count Raymond II gave the order the land in the early 1140s in the crucial Buqaia Valley, which linked Tripoli to the Muslim cities of the East. Controlling this route was very important for the Christians, and the Hospitallers proceeded to build one of the most formidable fortifications of that time in the so-called Buqaia Gap, which overlooked the valley and gave the Christians a good bastion of defense from the Muslims. A fortification had already existed in this area, and the order supposedly built the new castle upon its ruins. Fortunately, the castle has been preserved, so we can clearly see today the sheer challenge it posed to those who tried to take it. Such magnificent fortifications gave the Hospitallers a great defensive advantage since they were not as numerous as their enemies. Constantly manning the tens of castles scattered around the Holy Land and defending the vital points from Muslim attacks would slowly become one of the main responsibilities of the order, a responsibility it would nobly carry out for many decades.

Organization of the Order

Both the Knights Templar and the Knights Hospitaller were exceptionally well-organized institutions with a clear-cut set of rules on almost every aspect associated with running the orders. In fact, this level of organization was pretty difficult to find in other medieval-age establishments, let alone in ones that were constantly under threat of attack and destruction by hostile forces right on their doorstep. The effective coordination of regulations and practices made the knights of the two orders extremely disciplined and professional, traits that best manifested themselves when the Hospitallers and Templars fought side by side with other troops in the Latin armies. The discipline acquired by strictly following the orders' rules translated very well in military campaigns, as the knights would distinguish themselves not only by their bravery and skill but also by their dedication to orderliness and respect for the chain of command. Still, although the Hospitallers and Templars were mostly similar, they were different organizations.

In comparison to the Templars, the Knights Hospitaller never truly turned away from its origins of caretaking and providing help in hospices, even as the order became increasingly militarized throughout the 12th century. This meant that the roles of individual members needed to be clearly stated to ensure that things ran smoothly, especially as the order's services in Jerusalem grew exponentially in the years following the First Crusade, with St. John's hospital including about one thousand beds. Raymond du Puy is credited with the creation of the Rule of the Hospitallers, which was concerned with almost all aspects of the order's organization, including the division of labor and tasks, the chain of command, the everyday life of the brothers, admission, and punishments in case someone violated the rules.

The level of bureaucracy in the Knights Hospitaller is truly remarkable. As already mentioned, the grand master was the main leader of the order. He had the highest authority in the organization. He was essentially responsible for the order's general direction of development and oversaw the areas that needed his direct involvement. The fact that he was an elected knight from the order granted him a great deal of legitimacy, a detail that is very interesting in an age when status and rank were mostly determined by birth.

Below the grand master were several important individuals who each oversaw different aspects of the order's organization. The marshal was perhaps the second most important figure in the Knights Hospitaller, as he was responsible for everything associated with the military side of the organization. In the later years, once the order had grown enough to have its own navy, the role of admiral was created. An exclusively Hospitaller office was called the Hospitaller, an individual charged with running the order's hospices (there was no corresponding person for this in the Knights Templar). There were also regional masters who were in charge of the order's activities in the different regions of Europe, like France, England, and Iberia. Essentially, they acted like the grand masters of their areas but were subject to the grand master, who usually resided in Outremer. The Castellans were Hospitallers tasked with commanding individual castles under the possession of the order. The draper was a very interesting and respected individual; he oversaw the production of the order's uniforms and other garments. The treasurer was concerned with fiscal matters and bore many responsibilities, especially as the Hospitallers acquired more wealth.

The Hospitaller brothers followed a strict hierarchy. Since every Christian male could realistically be admitted to the order (even former serfs and men from lower-ranking families could join as long as they were dedicated enough), this meant that theoretically everybody could rise up in the ranks to become the grand master, although, of course, some held more advantages. Usually, after a person was received by the order and underwent a formal ritual where they pledged allegiance to the order for life, they would either become a knight, a sergeant, a chaplain, or a squire based on their rank, will, and experience.

The knights were the highest-ranking of ordinary brothers. They were mostly experienced warriors or knights and came to the order from Europe, seeking glory by fighting and dying in the name of God. Wearing the iconic black uniforms with the white cross, they were the most elite units the order fielded. When they rode into battle, they wore a chainmail tunic and a padded undergarment below their attire, as well as durable leather boots, all of which were provided to them by the draper's office. Sometimes, the knights wore a metal pot helm to protect their heads. The helm had a tight slit for their eyes and nose. However, many preferred to fight with only a chainmail cap that did not cover their faces due to the heat in Outremer.

The weapons wielded by the brothers varied based on preference, but most of them used either a broadsword or a mace with a shield and lances when they were mounted. The knights were also given a specially-bred horse, a carefully chosen destrier that would become their companion throughout their time in the order. The knights' horses were dressed similarly to the brothers who rode them, sometimes even wearing armor that made the mounted Hospitallers heavy shock cavalry. Of course, each knight had one or two personal squires, who were younger, usually lower-born members of the order. They aided the knights.

Below the brother-knights were brother-sergeants and chaplains. The sergeants were also mainly from lower-born families. Although they took part in military activities, they usually specialized in distinct fields, like blacksmithing, cooking, building, taking care of the stables, and much else. Sergeants did not get as many privileges as the knights, but with enough dedication and hard work, they could distinguish themselves and climb the ranks. They served a role in the day-to-day activities of the order, although by the end of the 12th century, most sergeants actually operated in the order's European possessions. The chaplains, on the other hand, were Hospitaller priests, and they never engaged in military campaigns. They helped run the churches associated with the order, read sermons, and offered other religious services to the brothers. Interestingly, in the early days of the hospital, volunteer women were admitted to the order. They either became nuns or nurses and were confined to the hospices. This was drastically different from the Knights Templar, where only men were allowed from the very beginning. As time went by, the ranks of the Hospitallers started being dominated by men.

The Fall of Edessa

For a while after the First Crusade, things were going relatively well for the Latin kingdoms, something in which the Hospitallers played an increasing role. The Muslim raids were pretty difficult to deal with at first, but they did not really lead to significant domination over the Christians. The main reason behind the Christians' early success after 1099 has to be attributed to the relative weakness of their foes instead of any good strategy adopted by the Latins. Although the crusaders made some advances after capturing Jerusalem by taking small pieces of land to ensure better connectivity between their conquered territories and establish better naval links through the Mediterranean ports in Outremer, they were not seriously opposed for the first thirty years in their endeavors.

Beginning in the late 11th century, the Muslim world entered a brief period of disarray, and the height of Muslim instability coincided with the First Crusade at the end of the century, where the Muslims would be overwhelmed by the crusaders. The Fatimid Caliphate, which was based in Egypt and North Africa but also had its eyes on Syria and Palestine, was constantly under fire from the Sunni Seljuk Turks, who were constantly wrestling them for the control of key cities in the region like Damascus and Baghdad. The truth of the matter was that the Fatimids had never seen such a formidable foe as the Seljuks, and their defeats in the military confrontations between the two resulted in an unstable empire. This was also followed by a succession of weak caliphs in the realm's capital, Cairo. These caliphs were constantly challenged by the growing power of the caliphate's regional lords.

Thus, in the first years of the 12th century, with the five-year-old al-Amir on the throne, it is unsurprising the chaos was slowly becoming uncontrollable. The caliph was essentially only in charge of a small area surrounding Cairo. Court intrigue, murder, and the ambitions of independent emirs caused a great deal of decentralization in the caliphate. This was why the Fatimids were unable to produce an effective answer after the conquest of Outremer by the Latins.

The Seljuk Turks were the more dominant Muslim force in the region in the late 11th and 12th centuries. Thanks to their formidable, bloodthirsty warriors, who believed they were fighting a holy war for a purpose and were masters of mounted combat, the Seljuks had managed to sweep westward from central Asia, decimating whatever resistance they encountered on their way, including the Byzantines at Manzikert in 1071. Strong Seljuk sultans in the 11th century (Tughril, Alp Arslan, and Malik Shah) guaranteed the success of the Turks and made them a feared enemy of the Byzantines. But after the passing of Malik Shah in 1092, the Seljuk Empire showed its weakness as well, as it was not as good when it came to administration and governance as it was at war. The successors of Malik Shah were all weak compared to their predecessors, and the First Crusade came as an additional shock to them. All of this caused instability among the Seljuks, whose princes started quarreling among themselves for control of the empire.

Still, even though the 12th century started out relatively well for the crusaders, they were unable to sufficiently consolidate their power in the region, something that stemmed from the lack of manpower and personal disagreements between the leaders of the kingdoms. The first real challenge the Christians of Outremer experienced came in the 1130s in the form of a slave-turned-atabeg (Seljuk provincial governor) by the name of Zengi. Zengi managed to become the atabeg of Aleppo and Mosul and was notorious for hating Christians and his dedication to expelling them from Outremer, which he believed belonged to the Muslims. In addition to his charisma and jihadist calling, Zengi was also well known for his ruthlessness and unusually cruel nature. The records of the time depict him engaging in terrible activities against his enemies, including torturing captured troops by scalping and skinning them alive. Castration was another one of the measures he usually resorted to, for instance, if he disliked the conduct of his subordinates. Since the Seljuk lord enjoyed such dreadful methods, he instilled fear in his enemies and allies alike, which even resulted in a fellow atabeg of Damascus, Mu'in ad-Din Unur, turning to Jerusalem for a temporary alliance against Zengi (in fact, Unur's legation upon their travels to Jerusalem noted the noble demeanor of the Hospitallers and the Templars, among other fine things the Holy City had to offer).

Throughout the 1130s, Zengi consolidated his power and united some of the regional Muslim warlords under his banner, giving him firm control of Aleppo and Mosul—two very important cities in Syria. The Byzantines, under John II, even wanted to take Aleppo for themselves, but they were dissuaded in 1138 after learning that Zengi had captured the city. Still, the atabeg was reluctant to strike the Latins just yet, so he waited for a good opportunity, which presented itself in the early 1140s after King Fulk of Jerusalem passed away after falling off his horse. This left the most powerful Latin kingdom in the hands of his twelve-year-old son, Baldwin III, with his mother, Melisende, as regent in 1143. John II of Byzantium, a rare Byzantine emperor who cooperated with the Catholic crusaders, also died in the same year.

This subtle instability was enough for Zengi and his men, who had already started raiding the small Christian towns and villages that were unprotected in the northern part of the Latin kingdoms. In 1144, the atabeg of Mosul led his men to the city of Edessa, a glorious city and the capital of the County of Edessa, which at the time was headed by Joscelin II. The young and inexperienced Joscelin had just lost two of his main allies, and a personal quarrel with Raymond II of Tripoli basically left him defenseless against the Muslims. The count did try to gather up whatever forces he had in late 1143 to try and take Aleppo and stop the inevitable incursion of Zengi, but the two armies missed each other. Before the Christians could besiege the seat of the atabeg, they heard the news that Edessa had fallen in late 1144.

The Fiasco of the Second Crusade

Count Joscelin II wisely did not attempt to recapture Edessa right away, knowing that the Muslim army was much larger than what he had. Instead, he decided to retreat from Aleppo and evade Zengi for as long as he could. He was desperate for help from his fellow crusaders. The news of Edessa's fall spread quickly throughout Outremer and Europe; after all, Edessa had been one of the most important cities in the Holy Land. The Crusader States realized their mistake of being reluctant to help Joscelin and tried to make it up by sending dignitaries to Rome to ask for help.

Although over four decades had passed since the capture of Jerusalem, the crusading spirit was by no means dead in mid-12th-century Europe. Several minor expeditions had been attempted to reinforce the ranks of the crusaders with fresh men who were willing to fight, and the newly created Catholic military orders (the Templars and the Hospitallers) certainly amplified the desire to go to the Holy Land. In addition, the *Reconquista* was still actively going on in Iberia, and the existence of Muslims right at Europe's doorstep made the calls for another crusade even more realistic. Eventually, the Second Crusade would be called in December of 1145, thanks to the efforts of Bernard of Clairvaux and Pope Eugenius III.

This time, the campaign would be led by King Louis VII of France and King Conrad III of Germany, who managed to assemble about forty thousand men with the intention of traveling to Outremer and reclaiming Edessa from the heathen Zengi. (The Second Crusade also involved two other expeditions: one directed at the Muslims in Iberia, where the Catholic Iberian kings heavily relied on the Templars and Hospitallers to achieve success, and one directed at the pagan Slavic people (the Wends) living in northern Germany. This crusade was led by several German princes and is also referred to as the Wendish Crusade. Ultimately, both of these campaigns would prove to be far more successful than Louis's and Conrad's expedition to Outremer.)

Although hopes were high, with everyone expecting a triumphant crusade like the first one, the expedition encountered more difficulties and would turn out to be one of the most poorly coordinated crusades. The main problem was that it took more than a full year to assemble the armies and plan the route to get to the Holy Land, during which time the situation in Outremer had somewhat changed. For example, in 1146, after returning to Mosul from Edessa, Zengi was assassinated by one of his men, and the command of the atabeg's forces was transferred to his son, Nur ad-Din. Following Zengi's death, Joscelin II tried to retake his capital in October 1146 and managed to reach and hold the citadel for a few days, after which he was confronted by Nur ad-Din's forces and was forced to retreat.

Also, the two kings did not wait for each other to start the campaign. Louis VII, who was a very pious monarch, had long been planning to see the Holy Land for himself. In a way, he treated the expedition as his own personal pilgrimage. He set out on his journey in early June 1147 from Paris after a ceremonious goodbye from the assembled nobles and clergy. Conrad III was rather reluctant to join the Second Crusade in the first place. He embarked on his journey about one month later than the French. One could notice from the way the crusade had begun that not all was hunky-dory for the crusaders.

One hurdle the crusaders encountered on their journey showed itself once they got to Constantinople. The crusaders asked Byzantine Emperor Manuel I to let them pass to Outremer through Anatolia. However, Manuel I was not as keen on the Catholics as some of his predecessors and was not content that two massive armies were encamped in his lands. In fact, the crusaders most likely terrorized the Byzantine countryside as they approached the capital, taking away the locals' resources to keep the expedition going. The fact that they presented themselves as fighters for Christendom was unacceptable to the emperor, who believed that it was the Orthodox Byzantines who had been fighting against the Muslims for hundreds of years.

Thus, while the pious King Louis dined with Emperor Manuel I to negotiate the pass of his forces and actually made a good impression, King Conrad went ahead impatiently with his twenty-thousand-strong army, rushing through the center of mountainous Anatolia to get to Outremer. His decision would prove to be fatal for the Germans. In October, the Germans were ambushed at Dorylaeum by the Seljuks, and only an estimated tenth of the original army survived, including a wounded Conrad, who just managed to save his skin. Conrad and his men retreated to the Byzantine city of Nicaea and reluctantly joined up with the French. However, Conrad had to stay behind due to illness. Eventually, he and his small company sailed to the city of Acre from Constantinople, from where he would finally get to Jerusalem in 1148.

Meanwhile, King Louis had been advised to take an alternative path through the southern Anatolian coast to get to the Holy Land, which, Manuel I had said, was much safer than going through the territories controlled by the Turks. Still, it is unclear whether or not the Byzantine emperor actually wanted the best for the French, as they struggled to get to Outremer because of constant light cavalry raids from the Muslims. The crusaders had to endure small-scale attacks almost every day throughout their journey to the coastal city of Antalya while having almost no means to effectively answer back.

Luckily, King Louis was also accompanied by a contingent of about one hundred Templar knights who had joined the Second Crusade in France. Thanks to the Templar efforts, namely their encouragement of discipline and professionalism, the expedition managed to get to their destination, though the men were still badly battered from the nonstop attacks. One could see the clear differences between the actions and conduct of the Templars and other French soldiers, the latter of whom would tremble at the sight of the enemy, break formation, and often desert during the night. If not for the brothers of the Templar Order, the campaign would have been wiped out, just like Conrad's army.

In the spring of 1148, the crusaders finally arrived in the Kingdom of Jerusalem, stopping at the city of Acre, where a council of Latins was called to discuss the next plan of action. However, as the crusader nobles showed up, they were disappointed to find that only a few thousand men from the original forty thousand had made it to Outremer. Still, the Council of Acre, which was held on June 24th, was a very important event. All of the major figures of the time attended it, including Conrad, Louis, King Baldwin III of Jerusalem, Supreme Patriarch Fulk, Queen Melisende, and, most importantly, Grand Masters Robert de Craon of the Knights Templar and Raymond du Puy of the Knights Hospitaller. Interestingly, no representatives from any of the other Crusader States (Antioch, Tripoli, or Edessa) were there to offer their input, indicating that Baldwin III wanted all of the glory for himself.

In the end, due to the vigorous efforts of King Baldwin and Templar Grand Master Robert de Craon, the council chose to attack the city of Damascus instead of journeying all the way north to Edessa. This was a surprising and somewhat illogical decision. Supposedly, Grand Master Raymond argued against it during the council but was eventually overruled. Not only was Damascus a heavily fortified city, but it was also not under the control of Nur ad-Din. The sudden change of plans seemed suspicious, to say the least. Nevertheless,

King Baldwin made the case that it was historically one of the core Christian cities, and the crusaders, reinforced by the knights provided to them by the Kingdom of Jerusalem, including a fresh contingent of Templars, started their move in late June. No records show that Raymond du Puy sent his fellow Hospitaller knights to aid the expedition.

The actual strength of the combined crusader forces at the time is unclear. Although some sources put it at around fifty thousand, it is very unlikely that they could have assembled this many men from Jerusalem alone. Conrad and Louis had, at best, a third of their original forces at their disposal, and even with Templars coming to aid the crusaders, King Baldwin could not have gathered tens of thousands of soldiers to fight.

In any case, the campaign to take Damascus was a total fiasco for the crusaders, who experienced a multitude of problems getting to the city in the extreme summer weather, with the ill-disciplined foot soldiers deserting along the way. By the time the crusaders got to the city and surrounded it, they chose the strategically worst position to attack from: through the deep marshes on the city's southern side. This spot made the crusaders prone to counter-maneuvers from the Muslims. Quarrel in the camp also plagued the crusaders, who were finally confronted and defeated by Nur ad-Din's relief force that had come to save their fellow Muslims by the end of July. The leaders of the Second Crusade were forced to call off the attack and return to Jerusalem empty-handed. The Second Crusade was a disaster, and the disappointed kings of France and Germany would sail back home a couple of months later, taking with them whatever men they had left.

The Siege of Ascalon

Despite the failure of the Second Crusade, King Baldwin III was nevertheless adamant about consolidating his position in Outremer, something he believed was even more essential due to the recent fiasco the crusaders had suffered at Damascus. However, instead of pushing for a retaliatory strike against Nur ad-Din and the Seljuks in the northeast, the king of Jerusalem set his eyes southwest on the relatively weaker Fatimid Caliphate. A few years after Damascus, Baldwin slowly started to rebuild his army and made some progress, rebuilding the stronghold at Gaza and entrusting its ownership to the Templars. The Templars significantly fortified Gaza to dissuade any

Fatimid raids. Only about ten miles from the Templar holding lay the city of Ascalon, a heavily fortified Fatimid outpost on the Mediterranean coast in modern-day Israel. Ascalon was a crucial fortress, as it allowed the Egyptians to launch disruptive raids into the crusaders' territory. Conquering Ascalon seemed like a logical next step in King Baldwin's mind. So, soon after the rebuilding of Gaza was done, preparations were made to take the city. The long siege of Ascalon would be one of the first large-scale battles in which the Knights Hospitaller would actively take part.

The siege of Ascalon was a massive campaign for Baldwin, who probably had more than five hundred professional Templar and Crusader knights and sergeants in his ranks, including the grand masters of both orders. The crusaders started the siege in late January 1153, hoping to starve the Egyptians inside the city walls and force a surrender. But the garrison in Ascalon, thanks to the city's access to the sea, managed to hold out for several months. Attrition significantly affected the crusader ranks. Efforts to cut off the city from the sea failed, and the siege was forcibly drawn out against Baldwin's will. By August, it seems the situation got too desperate for Baldwin. His ranks were reinforced by pilgrims, whose ships were deconstructed to be rebuilt as siege equipment for the city's walls.

As small-scale skirmishes broke out from time to time over the five-month-long siege, with the crusaders trying to storm the city with small numbers, luck would eventually save Baldwin from another humiliating defeat. In August, as the Muslim defenders were comfortably enclosed within the protection of the city walls, their efforts to burn down one of the siege towers supposedly backfired. The wind, which blew against the walls, pushed the debris from the tower back toward the garrison, resulting in a sudden collapse of a small portion of the city walls.

According to William of Tyre, this was seen as an opportunity by Templar Grand Master Bernard de Tremelay, who charged the opening with about forty of his knights, either as a genuine attempt to storm the defenders or as a short-sighted, gluttonous move to claim the glory of the city's capture. The Templars acted on their own without coordinating their plan of attack with the king. Although they fought valiantly and even made an advance past the city walls, they were ultimately outnumbered by the Egyptians, who massacred every single one of the brothers, including Grand Master Bernard. To send a message, the defenders then took the bodies of the slain Templars and hung them over the walls to terrify the Franks. In the morning, King Baldwin and the rest of his troops woke up to the horror of the hanging Templar bodies, but ultimately, the foolish sacrifice made by the Templars would not be in vain.

In fact, it was probably Grand Master Raymond du Puy who pressed the king to order a full-scale assault. He would have been angered by the disrespect the defenders had shown the Templars. Raymond du Puy was successful in convincing most of the army's officers and Baldwin himself, who ordered a heavy bombardment of the city, which weakened the defenses of Ascalon even more. Then, the Hospitallers, fighting alongside their remaining Templar brothers in the vanguard and leading the charge for the crusaders, stormed the city walls. The rest of the Christians followed. In a couple of days, on August 19th, 1153, Ascalon's defenders capitulated, giving the Latins a Pyrrhic victory. In a rare act of kindness and mercy, Baldwin III allowed the Muslim inhabitants of the city to evacuate peacefully, and the city was entrusted to the patriarch of Jerusalem, who had also accompanied the crusaders during the siege with a relic from the True Cross.

In the coming years, Ascalon would become a crucial outpost for Jerusalem, whose kings launched many invasions deep into Egypt. More importantly, the Hospitallers' bravery and open-mindedness earned the order many favors from the king, unlike the Templars, who, due to a bad decision from their grand master, returned home empty-handed.

Chapter Three – High Highs and Low Lows

Struggle for Egypt

Despite the victory at Ascalon, the Knights Hospitaller had to confront a much more difficult task: defending themselves against Nur ad-Din in the north. In the years following the capture of Ascalon, the military core of the Hospitallers defended the northern Holy Land against the Seljuk ruler's continuous invasions. However, their efforts against Nur ad-Din produced mixed results, mostly due to the fact that the Catholic armies were constantly outnumbered by the Muslims. In February 1157, Baldwin III unwisely broke the peace treaty between Jerusalem and Nur ad-Din by ordering some of his men to disrupt Muslim trade in the region. This angered the Muslim leader, who renewed his assaults on Christian positions. He besieged the fortress of Banias, where he ambushed and overpowered the local Hospitallers, forcing their retreat from the region.

Then, under Humphrey II of Toron, the regional lord who controlled Banias and the surrounding areas and was also a constable of the Kingdom of Jerusalem, the Hospitallers fought against Nur ad-Din's forces on many other occasions. During the siege of Banias, which would eventually be relieved by Baldwin III in a rare act of mutual aid between crusaders, a contingent of Hospitallers fought in both Christian armies. Still, the surrounding areas of the castle were basically controlled by the Muslims, with the Hospitallers being fortified inside the fortress. Later on, the order would officially acquire control of the castle from Humphrey II, who desperately needed funds to govern his fiefdom. The fact that the Hospitallers were outright able to buy the castle again demonstrates their financial strength and independence during a period when resources were running thin for the crusaders.

It seems that sometime during this period, Raymond du Puy passed away. Auger de Balben succeeded him as the next grand master in 1160. Not much is known about Raymond's death. Some records even indicate that he visited Italy after the siege of Ascalon. Nevertheless, his tenure as the grand master can only be described as very fruitful, and he is considered to have been the man who laid the foundations for the order's future successes. Not much is known about Grand Master Auger either. He only held this role for two years until his death, with Gilbert of Assailly becoming the next grand master in 1162. Grand Master Gilbert was an experienced French knight, and under him, the order would pursue an even more active military role.

King Baldwin III died in February 1162 at the age of thirty-three. The ambitious king was succeeded by his brother, Amalric, the Count of Jaffa and Ascalon, as he had no children of his own. King Amalric was perhaps just as motivated to consolidate his position in Outremer as his late brother. He was experienced in fighting the Muslims during his tenure as count and firmly set his eyes on the Fatimid realm. A large-scale invasion of Egypt seemed logical in the early 1160s, as the ruling dynasty had many problems that affected its unity and strength, making it prone to internal divisions and incohesive governance between regional warlords. However, due to the lack of manpower and the difficulties that followed in the crusader States at that time, a campaign deep into enemy territory was perhaps not the wisest move.

In the ensuing campaigns to capture Egypt, the Hospitallers made up a central contingent of King Amalric's armies, as Amalric had developed a good personal relationship with Grand Master Gilbert. He played a big role in convincing the king to continue the attack on Egypt, which was suffering from dynastic struggles, even after the first campaign in 1163 had been abandoned due to the overflooding of the Nile. During this first attempt to conquer Egypt, the Hospitaller stronghold of Krak des Chevaliers came under attack from Nur ad-

Din's forces. Due to the superiority of the castle's defensive position, the order managed to halt the Muslim advance before a joint Frankish-Byzantine relief force arrived and achieved a rare decisive Christian victory at the Battle of al-Buqaia.

However, the relentless Nur ad-Din regrouped his forces and thrust into enemy territory once more, this time besieging Harim in the Principality of Antioch. Nur ad-Din was reinforced by his brother's forces from Mosul. The united Christian army, led by Raymond II of Tripoli, Count Joscelin III of Edessa, Bohemund III of Antioch, and Byzantine Emperor Konstantinos Kalamanos, followed Nur ad-Din to Harim. They were motivated by their recent triumph. They confronted the Muslim warlord in August and forced him to retreat.

However, the Christians' success appears to have been short-lived. They chased the retreating Muslim forces, who led them into a preplanned ambush, where Nur ad-Din slaughtered most of the Christian army. He captured the Christian leaders and killed thousands. It was a crushing result for the crusaders of Outremer, and to add insult to injury, Nur ad-Din moved in to finally take Harim and Banias in 1164, defeating the Hospitallers.

King Amalric pushed to conquer Egypt again a year later, in 1164, with the Franks backing a former powerful vizier named Shawar in the struggle for power. At Bilbeis, located northeast of the Fatimid capital of Cairo, the crusaders besieged hostile Egyptian forces in August, but the three-month-long siege ended in a stalemate after they were unable to find a breakthrough. Shawar's enemy, general Shirkuh, decided to ally with Nur ad-Din, asking the Syrian warlord to attack the crusaders in the north to dissuade following campaigns in the Nile Delta. Nur ad-Din obliged, and for the next two years, he sent several incursions into crusader territory, mainly pillaging the countryside and damaging communication and supply lines.

This made the crusader lords realize they needed more help from the military orders and prompted them to grant more lands and castles to the Templars and Hospitallers. Most of the fortresses in the northern County of Tripoli were entrusted to the Templars, and the order continued to man these castles until its last days. As for the Hospitallers, they received more than ten new holdings, including the magnificent Belvoir Castle in the Jordan River Valley, which would become one of the main pillars of defense against the Muslim incursions from the east in the following years.

Amalric's overzealousness to conquer Egypt showed itself once again in 1168 when Grand Master Gilbert again talked him into a renewed invasion of Egypt. The Crusaders had managed to achieve little on the Egyptian front, as the constant change of the balance of power and the difficult conditions for war proved to be problematic hurdles to overcome. Still, the five hundred Hospitaller knights and the same number of light cavalry provided by Gilbert for the campaign made an attempt too tempting to pass on. Thus, after nearly five years of campaigning, the king decided to push for Cairo. He even managed to reach the city by November 1168, although the men had been severely weakened by the constant small-scale attacks on their positions by the Egyptian light cavalry. The frustrated crusaders pillaged their way to the Egyptian capital, massacring the Muslim inhabitants and, as a result, alienating those Egyptians who were on their side. As the truce between Amalric and Shawar broke down, the invading crusader army was confronted by a relief force of about eight thousand men that was sent by Nur ad-Din from Syria. This army, led by Shirkuh, routed the already weakened Christians and forced them to abandon their advance on Cairo. Shirkuh's men managed to enter the city and emerge as the masters of Egypt.

The indecisiveness and impatience of King Amalric had cost the Christians yet another campaign in Egypt, while Shirkuh finally seized power in January 1169. The disappointed crusader army returned home to Jerusalem and had to confront the bitter reality. King Amalric was criticized for his willingness to negotiate with the Muslims, although his men's incompetence had led to the loss of the temporary alliance with Shawar (who would be executed by Shirkuh after his seizure of Cairo).

Ultimately, though, Gilbert of Assailly was mainly blamed for the unsuccessful campaign. A large majority of the Hospitaller forces had died during their multiple confrontations with the Muslims—a loss that was very difficult to swallow for the order. Gilbert was under pressure from within the order and from the Frankish nobles of Jerusalem. He was forced to resign his position as the grand master of the Knights Hospitaller and left Outremer for France. If nothing else, the multi-year campaigns in Egypt confirmed that the military orders were best utilized as defenders of the Holy Land, not as offensive tools.

Beware of the Warrior Monks

Although the campaigns in Egypt had been a disaster, the professionalism and skill of the military orders, both of the Hospitallers and the Templars, were duly noted by their enemies. Both orders were forged in battles with the Muslims, and it is unsurprising that their approach to life was also affected by them. Everyone had become aware of the bravery and valor of the brothers on the battlefield. And these men fully believed that they were guided in their endeavor to kill in the name of Christ by the sacred texts of Christianity. In fact, the "misinterpretation" of the scripture by the Templars and the Hospitallers was, to a large degree, intentional. Yes, Christ preached to uphold the principles of forgiveness and peace, but the military orders were motivated by their reading of the more violent Old Testament, which, in their view, justified killing the enemies of God.

As we have noted previously, perhaps going on the offensive against the Muslims was not a good move, at least strategically speaking, because of the objective lack of manpower and cohesion between the Crusader kingdoms. For those reasons, it would have been better for them to stay fortified in their castles and repel any incursions from the enemy. However, for the Templars and the Hospitallers, dying on the battlefield at the hands of the Muslims was equal to martyrdom, and they would rather be executed if they became prisoners. The warrior monks were feared in the Muslim world for their ascetic nature and dedication to their purpose.

By the end of the Egyptian campaigns in 1169, during the last of which the Byzantines had attempted to try and take the city of Damietta (albeit unsuccessfully), both of the orders' prestige and power had grown almost exponentially. It is hard to compare the scope of the two orders' activities because they were too similar in the endeavors they pursued. Still, it would not be an exaggeration to say that the Knights Hospitaller was the larger order of the two, at least when it came to possessions in Outremer. The Templars had focused a lot more on growing their order in Europe, especially in France and Iberia. This was because the Hospitallers were known for being more reserved, in general, than their Templar counterparts, who were perceived as being part of a more aggressive and famous institution with a solemn military tradition. For this reason, as well as for having a better network in Europe, the Knights Templar attracted more young men in search of their destiny and a path to eternal glory than the Knights Hospitaller. This is why the Hospitallers more frequently engaged in prisoner-of-war negotiations with their foes. When experienced knights were captured, the order could not afford to lose them and was prepared to pay a good sum of money for the release of senior knights.

Where we can more clearly observe the reserved and more open-minded nature of the Hospitaller Order is in its relationships with the Franks in Outremer. Count Raymond III of Tripoli was a man with whom the Hospitallers would find common ground. They would emerge as allies when the signs of instability between the Christians in the Levant started to show. The Hospitallers had been granted the possession of many castles in the County of Tripoli and were already on relatively good terms with the count, but the event that elevated their relationship to another level was when the order paid the ransom for Raymond in 1172 after the latter had been a prisoner of Nur ad-Din for about eight years.

Count Raymond was not a typical crusader; he was not motivated by the search for glory and hatred of his enemies. Instead, he was a well-read and disciplined man with an eye for strategy. He preferred peace to a war he knew the Christians would lose. Perhaps it was his wise nature that prompted him to forge a closer bond with the Hospitallers.

The relationship between Count Raymond and the Hospitallers demonstrated itself during the events of the 1180s when the Kingdom of Jerusalem was entangled in a succession dispute after the death of King Baldwin IV, also known as the "Leper King" due to his leprosy from which he had suffered since a young age. Upon his death in 1184, his infant son, Baldwin V, was supposed to become king, but he died in a year's time. Count Raymond had been appointed by the ailing Baldwin IV to be a regent for his son until the latter came of age to rule. But the high-ranking members of the Jerusalem court managed to manipulate the situation, basically limiting Raymond's influence in the kingdom's matters. To prevent Raymond from finding a suitable heir, perhaps even from a noble house in Europe, and solve the succession issue, Baldwin IV's sister, Queen Sibylla, gathered a coalition of powerful figures and married Guy de Lusignan, a noble French knight. She declared herself the queen and made Guy the king of Jerusalem in 1186.

The whole story of how Guy de Lusignan and Queen Sibylla manipulated the political situation in their favor is too complicated for us to discuss here, but it involved a great deal of help from influential individuals within the realm, including Patriarch Heraclius of Jerusalem, Count Joscelin III of Edessa, former Prince Reynald of Chatillon of Antioch, and the new Templar grand master, Gerard of Ridefort. All of these people had had some sort of personal disagreements with Raymond, and the count of Tripoli was only supported by Hospitaller Grand Master Roger de Moulins. Others blamed him for wanting to stage a coup and take power for himself.

Upon the accession of the new king and queen, each of these actors was granted gracious concessions. In an infamous incident, during the coronation ceremony of Guy de Lusignan, which took place in 1186, the royal insignia had to be unlocked from a coffer. One key for the lock was held by the patriarch, while the other two were in possession of the Templar and the Hospitaller grand masters. Roger de Moulins was approached on the day of the coronation to hand over the key. He chose to throw it out of his chamber window to show his protest against the newly proclaimed king and queen instead of breaking the oath he had taken as the grand master, which included carrying out this ceremonial responsibility.

Just like that, the relations between the Templars and the Hospitallers, two brotherhoods with the same goals but different means, started to slowly deteriorate at a very pivotal moment in the history of the Crusader kingdoms. This moment also amplified the severity of their growing resentment toward each other.

Saladin

It is also necessary to briefly mention the fact that the Crusader kingdoms had neither the time nor the resources to quarrel among themselves. The Egyptian campaigns had demonstrated that offensives deep into enemy territory would yield limited results for the Latins, so the expansion of their territories was not really an option.

There was another interesting development among the Muslims of Outremer that would soon prove to be a difficult challenge for the crusaders: the emergence of a disciplined and wise general who had formerly served alongside the Egyptian pretender Shirkuh against the Christians. His name was Salah ad-Din, referred to as Saladin by his Latin contemporaries—a name that would soon become illustrious in the medieval world. Saladin had helped Shirkuh gain power in Egypt and had even fought King Amalric and the Hospitallers several times, during which he had distinguished himself for his bravery and strategic eye.

In the early 1170s, when Shirkuh died soon after seizing power in Cairo, Saladin consolidated much of the former Fatimid territories, undermining the power held by the caliph, who had appointed him as his vizier. A devout Sunni Muslim, Saladin proceeded to fully abolish the Shi'a Fatimid Caliphate of Egypt in 1171, instead shifting his attention north to Syria while maintaining control of the Fatimid lands through his trusted generals. Three years later, after the death of Nur ad-Din in 1174, Saladin conquered much of Syria, overthrowing Nur ad-Din's successors and taking control of key cities like Damascus, Aleppo, and Baghdad. In 1175, after being proclaimed the sultan of Egypt and Syria, the Christians of Outremer perceived Saladin to be the biggest threat to their positions in the Levant, although they reluctantly came to acknowledge his skill and respect his wisdom as time passed.

Still, despite the power Saladin managed to amass during the years immediately following the death of Nur ad-Din, the first encounter between Saladin and the crusaders ended in a victory for the latter. In November 1177, Saladin, after having consolidated his standing in Egypt and much of Syria, launched an invasion of the Kingdom of Jerusalem. The sixteen-year-old Leper King, Baldwin IV, assembled whatever men he could and met the Muslim conqueror on the open field. Although the exact size of the two armies is unknown, Baldwin most likely had about three to four thousand men at his disposal, including contingents of the Templar and Hospitaller Orders. Saladin's forces outnumbered the Christians at least two to one. In what became a rare instance of a decisive Christian victory in the Levant, Baldwin's army was able to ambush the core of Saladin's forces, which were scattered over a large area. In the ensuing Battle of Montgisard, the Muslims were quickly routed due to their unpreparedness and were forced to retreat, suffering from many casualties in the process. Saladin himself is said to have just barely survived.

Of course, Montgisard would not be the final encounter between the Latins of Outremer and Saladin. For the next decade, the Muslim sultan clashed with the Christians over and over again. Eventually, by the mid-1180s, the situation between the two camps had stabilized a bit, with the Kingdom of Jerusalem even agreeing to a mutual truce. This was partly because of Saladin's poor health, which kept him from being as actively involved in his army's campaigns as he had been during his rise to power. Still, little by little, it was becoming obvious that the Latins would eventually be overpowered by the sheer numbers the sultan could field. And the first step toward defeating him would be addressing the existing issues within themselves.

However, the Latins saw no particular success on this front, as the events of the succession of Jerusalem after Baldwin IV's death basically split all of Outremer's Christians into two opposing factions, with the Hospitallers backing the alienated Count Raymond III of Tripoli. An interesting figure throughout the course of these events is Reynald of Chatillon, a French knight and an infamous individual in Outremer due to his hatred of the Muslims and his hot-headed nature.

Chatillon sided with Guy de Lusignan during the succession crisis in exchange for prestige and influence, which he used to basically pursue his own gluttonous interests. Interestingly, Chatillon would find a strange alliance with Templar Grand Master Gerard de Ridefort, during whose tenure the order would come to have increasingly bad terms with the Knights Hospitaller. The French knight, with the power and wealth he had accumulated in Outremer, even hired a pirate fleet in the Red Sea with the intention of getting to and pillaging the holy Muslim sites of Mecca and Medina, albeit to no success. Still, he made a name for himself due to his questionable character and ruthless attitude toward his enemies, the latter of which was certainly admired by the Templar grand master, who frequently sent brothers to aid Chatillon in his quest to exterminate all Muslims.

Reynald de Chatillon's actions would trigger the end of the truce between Saladin and the Christians in 1187 when he intercepted a Muslim caravan traveling from Syria to Egypt. He captured and tortured the defenseless merchants, despite calls from King Guy and Saladin to release the captives. This disrespectful behavior toward the weak angered Saladin beyond belief, and in March of 1187, he called a jihad on the Christians—a holy war against the Latins in Outremer. However, not all of the Christians were Saladin's enemies. Count Raymond of Tripoli managed to maintain relatively neutral relations with the sultan, and so had the Hospitallers, whose grand master, Roger de Moulins, only called for defensive action against the Muslims (though, admittedly, this was due to strategy, not the lack of resentment).

Thus, Saladin, who is seen as a gracious and responsible leader, approached Count Raymond with a proposition. He asked the count to let his forces march through his territories peacefully, saying that his target was Chatillon. Raymond agreed reluctantly, perhaps due to personal differences with Chatillon. But many in King Guy's court opposed the idea. The most fervent advocate against letting the Muslims pass was Grand Master Gerard de Ridefort. The Templar declared that he would rather die than allow the heathens to roam freely in Christian territories. Ultimately, he was overruled, but the high command agreed to send a joint Templar-Hospitaller contingent to scout enemy movements.

In early May 1187, as the Muslims started their march in the Lower Galilee region, about 150 Templars and Hospitallers in total (including both grand masters) closely surveyed their movements at night. From a nearby hill, the scouts spotted the Muslim army, which numbered around seven thousand troops, at Cresson Springs near Nazareth. Supposedly, Roger de Moulins believed that the best course of action was to get the word about the Muslims to Jerusalem, but upon seeing the enemy, Templar Grand Master Gerard de Ridefort swiftly got on his horse and charged downhill toward the Muslims, encouraging his troops to follow him. De Moulins saw his fellow grand master ride into battle and did not want to abandon his brothers. So, he reluctantly got on his horse, with the Hospitallers following him.

Thus, in yet another act of overzealousness and perhaps uncontrollable drive to die in battle as martyrs for Christendom, more than one hundred knights rode into the open arms of several thousand enemies. The result was catastrophic. Roger de Moulins, who had been dragged into the whole thing by his honor against his will, was slain in the small battle that ensued. Templar Marshal James de Mailly died fighting on his horse, surrounded by a swarm of Muslims. Gerard de Ridefort survived the suicidal charge and managed to flee the battle badly wounded. He reached the town of Nazareth, where he got the necessary help to stay alive.

Cresson Springs was a disaster, and the military orders were not able to inflict as many casualties on the Muslims as they would have liked. Saladin's victorious forces put the heads of the slain brothers on their pikes, sending a message to the Christians. Due to the foolishness of the Templar grand master, more than a hundred of Outremer's best troops had been killed, but back home, the scapegoat appeared to be Raymond of Tripoli. He was accused of treachery because he had let the Muslims enter Christian territory. As a result, he publicly pledged to have no more contact with the Muslims. He cut off all relations and fully joined King Guy's camp. This incident further strained the relations between the two orders, as well as between Raymond and the rest of the nobility of Jerusalem, including Reynald de Chatillon, who still had not been punished for his careless actions against the neutral Muslims.

The Fall of Jerusalem

After Cresson Springs, the main Muslim army went home, only to return with even more men and Saladin at its head in June. With an estimated number of thirty thousand troops in total, Saladin's blood-hungry force was ready to clash with the Christians. Saladin led his men near the Sea of Galilee, hoping to lure the Latins in and ambush them. As word of Saladin's return spread in the kingdom, King Guy managed to gather a force about half the size of Saladin's, including, of course, both Hospitaller and Templar contingents. Adding to their numerical disadvantage, the crusaders also had to confront the obvious problem within their camp: the problem of mutual hatred among some of the most important factions.

Not only were the Hospitaller and Templar knights resentful of each other, but Count Raymond, who had reinforced the king with his troops, was also on terrible terms with Reynald of Chatillon. Raymond believed that Saladin's renewed invasion had been caused by Reynald. The crusader army was split into three parts: the Hospitallers, along with Count Raymond, were in the vanguard; following them was the unfortunate King Guy, who was trying to hold his forces together with the might of the True Cross in the brutal sun of Galilee in late June;

and the Templars constituted the rear of the marching formation.

Saladin acted quickly and decisively, capturing Tiberias, which lay on the coast of the Sea of Galilee. Incidentally, the wife of Count Raymond, Eschiva, was also stuck in the city, although Saladin had left her and her personal guard in the city's citadel unharmed. The Muslim commander knew that the crusaders would be drawn to him because of her, and he was right. However, Count Raymond did not seek to hasten the army's advance to save his wife as soon as he could, although he did love her very dearly. There were about ten miles between Tiberias and the crusaders, and ten miles was a lot of distance to cover in the scorching summer heat. But when the count suggested playing a waiting game, he was again accused of being a traitor and a coward by most of the king's court. Still, at the end of the day, it seemed as if he managed to persuade King Guy to approach the matter cautiously and not rush toward Saladin. Despite this, the king had never been known for having a strong character. Templar Grand Master Gerard de Ridefort returned to the battlefield and managed to change the king's mind. The matter was thus decided.

It is perhaps difficult for anyone to imagine the march that ensued the next day, as the Christian camp was ordered to move ahead swiftly. Wearing full-body chainmail armor, carrying heavy swords and shields, and with no clean water source in their vicinity, more than fifteen thousand crusaders started their journey in the extreme summer heat to Tiberias. The troops struggled, reluctantly dragging their feet in the barren lands. They reached a ridge with two peaks near the village of Hattin, which was called the Horns of Hattin by the locals. King Guy was exhausted and dehydrated from the journey, so he ordered the army to camp there and rest as nightfall approached. Supposedly, Count Raymond, who knew that the army was stretched over difficult terrain and prone to enemy attacks, struggling from heat and dying of thirst, exclaimed, "We are dead!"

As the crusaders settled down for the night, Raymond's exclamation came true. Saladin's army, which was much larger and better prepared, descended upon the ranks of the Christians at dawn, not allowing them to get their much-needed sleep. The Muslims attacked the rear of the crusader army. Guy knew they were fighting a fight they would lose and ordered a retreat through the side of the ridge Raymond and the Hospitallers had encamped on. However, the

Muslim general had been prepared for this, as he ordered his men to set fire to the barren dry grass, setting the surrounding areas of the Horns ablaze and cutting off the crusaders' escape route.

The Hospitallers were forced to join the battle, and they actually managed to force their way through in the north toward the Sea of Galilee, fighting through hordes of Muslims. However, King Guy was stuck in the back and called for their assistance, urging the order to return after they had broken through to defend the True Cross. Still, it was too late. The Christians had been broken by Saladin's mightier army. Raymond acknowledged defeat and managed to flee westward to Tripoli, leaving behind his men. He was likely frustrated that he could not get his king to listen.

The crusaders suffered a crushing defeat at the Battle of Hattin. Most of the Christians were outright slain on the battlefield. Those who survived and fled were chased down by the Muslim light cavalry and captured. When Saladin got word that King Guy and Reynald of Chatillon had been captured, he fell on his knees with tears in his eyes, praising God's glory and thanking him for aiding the Muslims in the battle. The truth of the matter was that Saladin had just outsmarted and outfought the much weaker Guy and had consequently gotten his prize. Saladin could finally have his revenge on Reynald, who had terrorized the region's Muslims since his arrival in Outremer during the Second Crusade. After the two prisoners had been brought to him, Saladin proceeded to treat King Guy as respectfully as he could, telling him that "real kings did not kill each other" and offering him a seat beside his side.

Perhaps there was a small chance that the Muslim leader could have shown mercy to Reynald, but the latter continued to behave irresponsibly in his captivity, disrespecting Saladin and his religion. After Reynald rejected the sultan's offer to convert to Islam, Saladin supposedly unsheathed his sword and cut off his prisoner's arm before ordering his men to execute him for the evil and trouble he had brought upon all Muslims. Gerard de Ridefort was also captured by Saladin, along with dozens of Templars and Hospitallers. Gerard was kept alive since he was a valuable hostage; the Muslims knew that the order would pay a great sum of money for his freedom. The rest of the brothers were swiftly executed.

The Battle of Hattin was Saladin's first step in his subsequent conquest of most of the Christian-held Outremer. The bulk of Jerusalem's forces had been destroyed, and no one was left to meet the Muslims in an open battle. Saladin split apart his forces since he was unafraid of any resistance. He took Outremer's cities one by one throughout the summer. Many garrisons surrendered without fighting. Acre, Jaffa, Ascalon, and Nablus were all captured by Saladin in the months following his victory. Throughout all this time, King Guy remained in captivity, which caused even more chaos in Jerusalem, which was essentially left without a competent ruler. By late September, virtually all of the major cities and castles were under Muslim control, except the port city of Tyre due to its magnificent fortifications, as well as the Hospitaller castles of Marqab and Krak des Chevaliers and the Templar castle of Tortosa. Saladin purposefully avoided a head-on assault on all of these forts, knowing that he would face stiff resistance from the garrisons.

Finally, there was the obvious cherry on the top: the city of Jerusalem itself, the most prized possession. The city had been under the rule of the Latins for nearly ninety years. Still, even the mighty walls of the Holy City were not enough to dissuade Saladin from claiming it, although he did send word to the garrison to try and negotiate the capture of the city peacefully. Balian of Ibelin, who commanded the garrison, tried to gather as many men as he could, even knighting teenage boys and giving them swords to fight the Muslims. For more than a week, the Latins in the city held out, but on September 29th, the Muslims broke through the walls. It was looking desperate for the garrison, which ultimately pleaded for surrender, with Balian of Ibelin negotiating the terms with Saladin himself. After much consideration, Saladin agreed to ransom the Christian inhabitants of the city for an egregious sum of money, which would eventually be paid in part by the church and the military orders. On October 2nd, as Saladin and his men triumphally entered the Holy City, tens of thousands of Christians were ordered to leave, unlike in the First Crusade, during which the crusaders ruthlessly exterminated almost all of Jerusalem's inhabitants. The Christian refugees either went to Tyre or Antioch.

By the end of 1187, the situation in Outremer had become desperate. With Jerusalem under Saladin's firm control, the

Christians were left in disarray. They still did not acknowledge that they should have been blamed for their lack of success in the Holy Land.

Chapter Four – Darkest Hour

The Crusade of Three Kings

The fall of Jerusalem in 1187 produced another shockwave in Europe, much like the fall of Edessa a couple of decades beforehand. After Pope Urban III received the grave news from Outremer, he reportedly died of a heart attack on the spot in October 1187. It would not take long for Rome to issue a bull that called for a new crusade to be launched to retake the Holy City. About a month after the city's capture by Saladin, the newly-elect Pope Gregory VIII issued *Audita tremendi*, in which he described the need for the Christian world to unite once again against a common enemy.

By then, the rather unfruitful Second Crusade was old, irrelevant news in Europe. A new generation of potential knights had grown up, just reaching the age where their lifelong dreams could be fulfilled. They had all heard and, in some cases, even witnessed the legendary heroes who had come back from their travels to Outremer. In addition, both the Templar and the Hospitaller Orders were very well known throughout Europe at that time. The youth were easily caught up in the crusading spirit, as many young men had hopes of attaining eternal glory by fighting against the "real" enemy in the Levant.

But past experiences had demonstrated something about a military expedition to Outremer. The men needed competent and influential leaders who would be not only able to field and command large armies but also be wise enough to make good choices throughout the campaign. In this regard, the crusaders would be very lucky. The first one to properly answer the pope's call was Holy Roman Emperor Frederick I, referred to as Frederick Barbarossa. After receiving the news of the papal bull, the emperor made an effort to resolve some of his existing differences with the German clergy and sent word to the local princes to join the campaign. In December of 1187, he held a meeting with his ally, King Philip II of France, convincing him to assemble an army for the Third Crusade, although Philip, at that point, denied the request due to the ongoing conflict he had with England.

The chronicle tells us that Frederick was very organized when it came to conducting an actual expedition. He set an exact time for preparations, which would take over a year and be concluded in April 1189. In the end, he assembled about ten thousand capable men, a big portion of which were well-equipped knights. Barbarossa set out from Germany in early May 1189, choosing to take a land path to Jerusalem through Hungary (where he was reinforced by an additional small force of about two thousand men) and the Byzantine Empire.

Frederick I was not the only major leader from Europe who embarked on the Third Crusade. It seems that his meeting with King Philip proved fruitful, as the French monarch agreed on peace with England's King Henry II in January 1188, just a month after his meeting with Barbarossa. Both monarchs agreed to put aside their differences and muster up armies to join the Germans on the Third Crusade. To finance this, they implemented new taxes on their population and greatly encouraged participation in the expedition. The military orders' headquarters in Europe likely provided financial support, and many European brothers joined the crusading armies from the very beginning.

Before the initial preparations could come to an end, Henry II passed away, but the new king, Richard I, was perhaps an even better fit to lead the crusade. Richard I was a true soldier. He had a great hunch for strategy and decision-making and was adamant about going on the journey to Outremer. The two kings set out on the Third Crusade from the French town of Vezelay in early July 1190, about a year after Barbarossa had already embarked on his own expedition. Each of them had probably just short of ten thousand men at their disposal.

The Third Crusade was perhaps the most organized of all the expeditions so far, and it looked promising from the beginning for that reason. With two kings and an emperor as its leaders, there was an expectation that the mighty armies would emerge triumphant in the end. However, the Third Crusade would ultimately be plagued by a multitude of problems. In some instances, the Christians would just get outright unlucky despite their careful planning and set goals. The clearest example of this is Frederick Barbarossa, whose force marched through the lands of Hungary and the Byzantines. In Anatolia, Frederick was confronted by hit-and-run attacks from the Turkish Sultanate of Rum, although they had agreed to a truce before the start of the expedition. Still, the Germans crushed the Turks on different encounters, first at the Battle of Philomelion in May 1190 and then at the sultanate's capital city of Iconium, where the crusaders celebrated their decisive victory by sacking the city.

After these victories, the Germans suffered one of the most infamously unlucky incidents of the medieval era. As Frederick Barbarossa was crossing the Saleph River in southern Turkey, his horse slipped. The emperor fell into the river and drowned. This event would greatly demoralize the crusaders, many of whom packed up and returned home to Germany, perhaps believing they had already achieved a lot by defeating the Turks at Iconium. The emperor's son, Frederick VI, Duke of Swabia, would de facto lead the remaining forces; there was about a half compared to the beginning of the campaign. Frederick of Swabia would safely get them to Antioch by the end of summer 1190.

Philip's and Richard's expeditions also did not go without problems. When the two armies met up in Sicily, having agreed to set sail from there after separating from their original starting point of Vezelay, Richard I broke his betrothal to Philip's half-sister, Alys, instead deciding to marry the Spanish princess Berengaria of Navarre. This angered the French king, who fell out with Richard over the matter and set sail to Outremer alone, arriving in Tyre in April 1191.

The English crusaders started to set sail after Philip had already arrived in Outremer, and they suffered greatly on their way due to a heavy storm that forced them to stop at Cyprus. While there, Richard I had a disagreement with the Greek ruler of Cyprus, Isaac Doukas Komnenus, after the latter grew tired of the crusaders in his lands.

Richard eventually took the city of Limassol by force. After having essentially captured Cyprus (and still being on terrible terms with the French), Richard I and his crusader army finally arrived in Outremer in early June.

The first major military action of the assembled crusader forces would be the siege of Acre, an endeavor started by the Franks of Outremer in 1189. The siege had persisted for nearly two years. The European crusaders would learn of the ongoing siege when they arrived in Outremer and would join the effort one by one. First, the remaining Germans, now under Leopold V of Austria, who had taken over after the death of Frederick of Swabia due to illness, would join the cause. Then, in April 1191, King Philip joined his army. Finally, Richard I arrived at Acre in early June.

After the Englishmen's arrival, the siege really kicked off, with Richard taking charge of the preparations, which mainly included organizing the soldiers into different divisions and building siege equipment. Acre would fall into the hands of the crusaders after a bit of fighting in early July. Despite their victory, the crusaders at Acre still quarreled over who should be put in charge. This eventually caused Philip II, who was already on bad terms with the rest of the leaders and had been reluctant to join the expedition from the very beginning, to set sail to France, abandoning the Third Crusade even though Jerusalem had still not been taken. He was swiftly followed by Leopold of Austria. Many of the soldiers accompanied their leaders on their quest to return home. Only a couple of thousand men from the French and German armies agreed to stay and fight under the command of Richard. It was clear that the English king had a difficult task ahead of him.

Hospitallers Triumph at Arsuf

After the events of the siege of Acre, the Hospitallers really became involved in the Third Crusade, managing to play a significant role in the ensuing occurrences. A Hospitaller contingent was most likely present at Acre, although the order's role increased significantly after Richard I assumed total control of the remainder of the crusader army after Acre. The next target was the port city of Jaffa, whose control was crucial for a successful strike on Jerusalem. As Richard organized his forces, more than a hundred knights from both military orders joined the king, with the Hospitallers making up the rear while the Templars led the formation as the vanguard.

The march to Jaffa in the heat of the late summer sun was very difficult. To avoid being exposed to constant harassment from the open plains of the region, Richard tried to move on the coastline, knowing that at least one of his flanks would be protected by the Mediterranean Sea. Despite this, the hit-and-run attacks from the light horsemen of the Ayyubids still plagued the crusaders throughout their march, but thanks to the discipline enforced by the military orders, the soldiers barely broke formation, fending off the Muslims on multiple occasions.

Finally, after more than ten days of a difficult trek, the crusaders encountered a very menacing-looking Muslim force as they crossed the Rochetaillee River near Arsuf. The Muslims had approached the crusaders from the rear-left flank, and it was clear they were there to outright end the Third Crusade. It seemed that Saladin had taken the initiative into his own hands, as he personally led this mighty army to stop the crusaders' advance. The exact strength of Saladin's army is unclear, although some estimates suggest that his force was about twice as large as Richard's.

Although Richard spotted the Muslims at dawn on September 7th, he was reluctant to march his men into battle, knowing that his objective was to capture Jaffa. Engaging in an all-out battle with the Muslims would not have been a wise choice since the crusaders would have suffered many casualties. So, Richard ordered the column to stick together and to continue the march, at least to Arsuf, whose orchards would provide a better defensive position for an all-out battle. Still, the English king had little time to react, as the Muslims charged at the sight of the enemy, blowing their horns, banging their drums, and shouting their battle cries to intimidate the crusaders. Richard's army quickly organized into a tighter formation and braced for the first charge, although it certainly came as a shock, affecting the fighting morale of the crusaders.

The Hospitallers, who were at the back, were hit very hard since they were isolated from the rest of the more professional corps of the army, which was at the front of the column. During the chaos that ensued, Hospitaller Grand Master Garnier de Nablus managed to reach the king at the front, asking him to order a counter-attack so the brothers could answer the enemy charge. However, Richard was hesitant, as he did not want to break the formation. As it was, the crusaders had somehow withstood the initial charge of the Muslim cavalry, and their backs were still defended by the sea. The Hospitaller grand master was enraged when Richard demanded that he show the restraint and resilience for which the order was known. However, Richard's words would not be enough to dissuade Grand Master Garnier, who had already made up his mind.

Garnier de Nablus returned to his men in the rear amidst the heavy archer fire that descended on the crusader ranks. Garnier saw his men filled with zeal, crying out to take vengeance on the Muslims. Although he tried to communicate the king's orders, it was too late. Several Hospitaller knights had already broken through the lines, charging viciously at the enemy. Soon, the whole of Richard's rear was in deep hand-to-hand combat with the Muslims before the king realized what was going on. When he looked back, the Hospitallers and the knights who had followed them into battle had already cut through a lot of the resistance, forcing the king to change his approach and swiftly join his men in the rear.

Thus, the crusaders engaged in a massive counter-offensive, with the king proceeding to demonstrate his skill in battle. The counter-charge threw Saladin and his men off-guard, and the Muslims soon started to flee. Surprisingly, the Christians' bold move worked. Before long, Saladin's army was in full retreat, with thousands slain on the battlefield.

After the Third Crusade

Despite Richard I's decisive victory at Arsuf, the Third Crusade would not accomplish its main goal of recapturing Jerusalem for the Christian world. We will not cover how the expedition continued after Arsuf since it would require us to go into great detail about a topic in which the Knights Hospitaller were not involved, at least not to the same extent. Still, it has to be mentioned that the Third Crusade would not completely end in a disaster, thanks to Richard's eye for strategy, resilience, and the morale he inspired in his troops. For nearly a year after forcing Saladin to flee back into the safety of Jerusalem's walls, Richard would go back and forth, trying to gain control of as much land in the former crusader territories as possible. The English king even thought about launching a head-on assault on Jerusalem in 1192, but by that point, he correctly realized that he would be pushing his exhausted men too far. After months of smaller skirmishes between the crusaders and the Muslims, where neither side was ready to commit everything to defeat the other, Richard was able to achieve a sort of diplomatic victory with Saladin, who could not break the spirit of the crusader king.

On September 2nd, 1192, Richard and Saladin agreed on the Treaty of Jaffa, signing a three-year truce between the Christians and the Muslims. According to the terms of the peace, the city of Jerusalem would stay under Muslim control, but the Christian pilgrims would be allowed free passage throughout Palestine and access to the city, with Saladin personally guaranteeing their safety. In addition, the treaty also confirmed that the Christians would be granted the possessions of Tyre and Jaffa, as well as other towns in the area the Third Crusade was able to capture.

All in all, the Third Crusade was a semi-successful campaign. The crusaders would not be left completely empty-handed after 1192, but the problems that had plagued them before still needed to be addressed after the end of the campaign. After all, the treaty only guaranteed three years of peace with the Muslims, which was not nearly enough time to consolidate their position in Outremer to fight for the Holy Land. Richard I, who would attain the nickname "Lionheart" due to the bravery and skill he displayed during the Third Crusade, left Outremer soon after the treaty, leaving the Holy Land in the hands of the weak kingdoms and the military orders.

This instability would manifest itself soon after the departure of Richard, who had tried to use his authority to resolve some of the issues between the Frankish lords of Outremer. Outremer's nobility had grown to increasingly dislike King Guy de Lusignan, believing that he lacked the legitimacy to the throne of the Kingdom of Jerusalem after his wife, Queen Sibylla, for whom he had been king consort, passed away during the Third Crusade. It did not help that Guy was almost the complete opposite of Richard. Guy lacked the charisma and charm that had earned the English king his status among his subjects. To try to help King Guy retain his authority and, in a way, guarantee at least some sort of stability in Outremer, Richard granted him control of the island of Cyprus, which he had taken on his way to the Holy Land.

The Knights Templar had bought the island from Richard for 100,000 bezants, 40,000 of which they paid the English king at once. However, soon after establishing themselves on the island, they came into conflict with the local Orthodox population and decided not to remain in charge of Cyprus in mid-1191. While the Templars retained the possession of some of the island, Richard would officially make Guy the king of Cyprus in 1192.

The period from 1192 to 1194 was one of the most chaotic for Outremer's Christian kingdoms, as it saw the power struggle between King Guy and his challengers to the throne of Jerusalem and Cyprus. These two years were rather confusing for the Hospitallers and the Templars too. It is not an exaggeration to say that the military orders became the strongest entities in Outremer during this time, especially as the rest of the Frankish nobility nearly ate each other alive. Fortified in their magnificent castles, the Hospitallers and Templars were, at least, much richer than other Christians of the land, something that is proven by the fact that the Templars were able to outright pay an egregious sum of money for the control of Cyprus. There is no mention of King Guy paying anything to Richard when the latter made him king.

The Hospitallers, although more modest in their aspirations, continued their existence, motivated by their goal to defend the Holy Land from Christendom's enemies. They mostly acted on their own, launching small-scale raids on Muslim positions even after the truce between the Christians and Muslims had been established. It has to be mentioned that the flow of enthusiastic men from Europe never stopped during this time, as both orders managed to grow their numbers by the end of the 12th century.

An interesting development that is worth mentioning here is the establishment of another Catholic military order in the late 12th century: the Teutonic Order. Just like the Hospitallers and the Templars, the Teutonic Order's exact origins and years of formation are unclear. It is believed that during the siege of Acre in the Third Crusade, some German merchants from Lubeck and Bremen, who had probably been part of Frederick Barbarossa's original crusading force, organized a field hospital to take care of the Christian soldiers at Acre. After the crusaders successfully took the city, they established the hospital in Acre, with Saint Mary as their patron, something that was approved by Pope Clementine III. Eventually, the German House of Saint Mary in Jerusalem (as the organization was officially called) would be militarized sometime between 1196 and 1198. The order was modeled after the Hospitallers and the Templars. The reason behind this was the fact that many Germans had arrived in the Holy Land after the capture of Acre, especially as the new Holy Roman emperor, Henry VI, was preparing to launch his own campaign to Outremer to reclaim the Christian lands.

Unfortunately, the emperor would unexpectedly fall ill and pass away in 1197, with much of the preparations already underway. A large number of Germans planned to return home from Outremer but were persuaded by the new king of Jerusalem and Cyprus, Amalric II, Guy de Lusignan's brother, who had assumed the throne after his heirless brother's death in 1194. However, he was struggling to consolidate his position due to the quarreling barons of Outremer. He proposed the Germans stay, offering them to join the Hospital of St. Mary in Acre, thus militarizing the order. Later on, the Teutons would receive official approval from Pope Innocent III, who granted the newly created order permission to use their iconic white tunic uniforms with black crosses. Over time, just like the Templars and the Hospitallers, the Teutonic Order grew in the Levant but would ultimately move its headquarters to Europe, where it would find great success, operating mainly in northern Germany and eastern Europe. It even established its own state along the coast of the Baltic Sea in the following centuries.

It also has to be remarked that at the turn of the 13th century, the rivalry between the Templars and the Hospitallers had not ceased, and the two orders continued taking opposing sides in the political quarrels of Outremer. Of course, on the battlefield, they still fought together for the same cause, but behind the scenes, each tried to undermine the other to increase its own prestige and influence. A good example of this is the conflict between the Principality of Armenia and the Armenian Kingdom of Cilicia, an Orthodox enclave in the southeastern part of Anatolia that bordered Outremer from the north.

Bohemond IV of Antioch had the backing of the Templars, who were more than willing to get paid to fight against the Orthodox Armenians. The Hospitallers had tried to dissuade Bohemond from waging war against a Christian nation amidst all the existing chaos that already plagued Outremer. They offered their help to King Leo II of Armenia. In fact, throughout its existence, the Hospitaller Order always tried to maintain amicable relations with the Orthodox people of the former Byzantine Empire and even condemned the infamous sacking of Constantinople by the Venetian crusaders during the shameful Fourth Crusade in 1204.

The situation got more complicated when the Shi'a Muslim sect of the Assassins, an independent mirror organization of the Catholic military orders, assassinated Bohemond's son, Raymond, at a church in Tortosa in 1213. Although no concrete evidence of potential Hospitaller involvement has been discovered, the order was accused of conspiring with the Muslim Assassins. Of course, Grand Master Garin de Montaigu denied all accusations, stating that it was shameful to even assume the Hospitallers had anything to do with the assassination. Still, the incident indicates that speculations about the order's questionable allegiances existed.

The Templars were also in a mutual alliance with the Republic of Venice, which had helped the order grow its business in Italy and provided the Templars with ships to better conduct its activities. It was around this time that the Templars also started to increasingly adopt fiscal responsibilities, lending out sums of money to suitable candidates from their rich castles in Europe and Outremer. They kept records that showed financial transactions and came up with a clever system that could be classified as the first bank of the medieval era. Once again, this monumental rise to power was also true for the Hospitallers, but the Knights of Saint John, unlike their Templar brothers, never engaged in fiscal activities on this scale. Instead, they always tried to stay true to their origins and provided hospice services to the needy.

The Hospitaller Order also seems to have undergone rigorous reorganization during this period, which included the modernization of and changing the order's almost one-hundred-year-old statute. The man responsible for this was Grand Master Fernando Afonso of Portugal, a distinguished and experienced knight whose tenure lasted from 1202 to 1206. Arriving in Outremer after taking part in the Reconquista, the grand master addressed some of the administrational issues within the order that we have already addressed in the previous chapters. For example, after the beginning of the 13th century, all of the brothers would be explicitly divided into three classes of fighting knights (including the lower ranks of the sergeants and their henchmen), chaplain priests who were only preoccupied with religious activities, and caretaker brothers who mostly spent their time in the order's hospices in different cities.

Desperation for Eternal Glory

Despite the relative growth of the Hospitallers in the 13th century and some successful raids and small-scale encounters with the raiding Muslims, the turn of the century saw much of Christendom continue to desperately struggle to maintain its position in Outremer. The almost fanatical obsession with the Holy Land had persisted for over a hundred years, and the Christians' recent failures to reassert their dominance in the faraway lands of the Levant had motivated more and more Europeans to strive for eternal glory. Despite the best efforts of Richard the Lionheart, the Third Crusade had managed to achieve little in terms of easing the pressure the Muslims exerted on the Christians in Outremer. However, the English king had recognized that the Latins' main problem, the reason they had almost lost everything that had been gained in the First Crusade, was their incompetence, greed, and jealousy to get more than what was possible. Upon noticing this, Richard tried to reconcile the quarreling lords of Outremer, even trying to make Guy de Lusignan a more authoritative figure by granting him control of Cyprus, but his efforts would eventually be proven insufficient.

We briefly mentioned the shameful Fourth Crusade, where the Catholic crusaders changed course and attacked already weak Byzantium. They sacked the city of Constantinople in 1204 and, in a way, contributed to the ultimate decline of the Orthodox Eastern Roman Empire, which happened about two and a half centuries later. Still, although everybody realized what a terrible failure the Fourth Crusade had been, most Europeans brushed it aside and, in about a decade's time, revived the crusading spirit. In 1217, the Fifth Crusade was launched, called by Pope Honorius III. Just like its predecessors, morale was high in the beginning, with King Andrew II of Hungary and Duke Leopold VI of Austria leading the initial expedition, along with several other provincial nobles from the Holy Roman Empire and France.

However, just as had been the case before, the campaign was disjointed and plagued by several difficulties. Andrew and Leopold arrived in Acre by sea in the autumn of 1217 after encountering and defeating a small Egyptian army on their way there. At Acre, they held a meeting, which was attended by Bohemond of Antioch; the grand masters of the Templars, the Hospitallers, and the Teutons; and John of Brienne, King Regent to Queen Isabella II of Jerusalem. The crusaders managed to take some fortifications along the Mediterranean coast by early 1218, by which point King Andrew believed that he had upheld the vow he had made to the pope and returned to Hungary, taking much of his army with him. Leopold also thought about returning home, but a new wave of German and Frisian crusaders under Oliver of Paderborn and William I of Holland convinced him to stay. Outremer's Christians devised a new plan to attack the Nile Delta—the heartland of the Ayyubid Sultanate. The coastal city of Damietta was chosen as the first target, which would open the way to the capital city of Cairo.

Thus, in May 1218, the crusader army, estimated to be about twenty thousand strong, landed in Damietta. Hospitaller Grand Master Garin de Montaigu was present with his contingent of a couple of hundred knights, who had put aside their differences with the Templars to join the Fifth Crusade. Thanks to the brave fighting of the crusaders and the clever tricks used by Christian engineers, the crusaders were able to make great advances by late summer.

After that, however, the crusaders would be joined by reinforcements under Cardinal Pelagius, an official papal legate and a very disagreeable man. He considered himself to be the real leader of the expedition. Upon his arrival, he pointed out to John of Brienne that he was not the real king of Jerusalem and asserted that he had the most authority as an official representative of the papacy. While the leaders disagreed, fierce fighting continued throughout early 1219, with the crusaders managing to take more and more land and eventually surrounding Damietta by the summer. Ayyubid Sultan al-Kamil's garrison at Damietta was exhausted and on the brink of defeat, and he was also facing internal problems in his kingdom. So, he offered a ceasefire to the crusaders in August. He proposed to cede control of Jerusalem to the Christians in exchange for them leaving Egypt.

It was a surprising proposal. John of Brienne and the majority of the crusader knights wanted to accept it, as they regarded Jerusalem to be their primary target. However, Pelagius was not convinced, as he believed that he had the upper hand. He demanded that the Muslims give up control of all the castles near the Holy City as well. This stubbornness angered al-Kamil, who refused to accept the counter-proposal. He let the city fall in late 1219. Still, Cardinal Pelagius saw it as a victory for the Christians and decided to wait a little while before pushing for Cairo—a move that was opposed by a large portion of the knights. William of Holland could no longer put up with Pelagius and abandoned the effort.

The crusaders held out at Damietta for about two years before the cardinal thought that they had recovered enough to continue the expedition up the Nile. In July 1221, after having received thousands of more reinforcements from Europe and with his army significantly larger than at the beginning, Cardinal Pelagius and the crusaders started their march to Cairo. On their way, the crusaders made a fatal mistake: they stopped to encamp at a place along the Nile that was prone to floods and overflowing. Although the Muslims were in an overall disadvantageous position, they opened up the sluice gates and redirected the river to the crusaders. In a short while, the might of the Nile devoured the ambitious Christians, who started to flee desperately back to Damietta. On their way there, they were plagued by the extreme summer heat and the Egyptian light cavalry.

In desperation, the Hospitallers and Templars tried to stop the Muslims from chasing down thousands of crusaders, but to no avail. Grand Master Montaigu was captured, along with other high-profile nobles from Outremer. Cardinal Pelagius realized he had been defeated and agreed to a humiliating peace with the Ayyubids, abandoning Damietta and establishing an eight-year truce with the Muslims. The Fifth Crusade was over.

Chapter Five – Abandoning the Holy Land

From Hattin to La Forbie

Throughout the 1220s, the situation in the Holy Land did not change for the better. In the former lands of the Kingdom of Jerusalem, the Christians only controlled a handful of territories, with the succession dispute still in the air. John of Brienne, the titular king of Jerusalem, traveled to Europe to seek assistance from the Christians, but to no avail. More interestingly, in the year 1129, he would give up his claim on Jerusalem, as he had been elected as a regent co-ruler of the Latin Empire in Constantinople, which had been established by the Fourth Crusaders after they took the city in 1204. Other lords of Outremer were involved in personal struggles against each other, as they held eternal grudges. However, they could not achieve anything significant against the real enemy. Deprived of manpower, they increasingly relied on the independent Templars and Hospitallers for military support. But the military orders had stretched their numbers thin as well, manning all of the important castles they held to hold off potential Muslim invasions.

Holy Roman Emperor Frederick II embarked on his infamous crusade to the Holy Land in 1128. Frederick was actually supposed to join the previous expedition with Leopold of Austria and Andrew of Hungary but was unable to proceed after falling ill with his already assembled army in Europe. An eccentric but nevertheless well-educated and curious man, Frederick ambitiously wanted to reclaim Jerusalem, and his campaign would be one of the most peculiar in crusader history. For his failure to uphold his vows during the course of the Fifth Crusade, Frederick was excommunicated by Gregory IX. But he still sailed to the Holy Land with his large army in June 1128. Before that, he met with the traveling John of Brienne and set up his marriage with John's daughter, Isabella II of Jerusalem.

Frederick II arrived in Acre in September of the same year. However, while a part of Outremer's nobles and the German Teutons happily received him, many important figures were reluctant to openly declare their support for the excommunicated king, the Hospitallers and the Templars among them. In addition, Frederick did not conceal his love for Eastern wisdom and Muslim culture, something that definitely played a role in the military orders' reluctance.

Soon after arriving, Frederick received word from home that Pope Gregory was angered by the actions of the proud emperor to launch a crusade while being excommunicated (and continuing a long history of hostilities between the papacy and the Holy Roman Empire). The pope was planning to invade his Italian territories. Thus, upon his arrival, Frederick realized that he could not stay in Outremer for long. After assessing the situation further, he concluded that fighting against the Muslims for territory would be useless.

However, against all odds, Frederick II managed to negotiate a surprising deal with the Ayyubid sultan, al-Kamil (the one who had been the reason for the Fifth Crusade's failure). With the Treaty of Jaffa, which was finalized in February 1229, the two sides agreed on a ten-year truce. Al-Kamil also agreed to cede the control of Jerusalem and the surrounding territories to the crusaders in exchange for the Christians taking care of Muslim sites that remained in the cities. This was a clear victory for Frederick, who, upon completion of the negotiations, triumphantly marched into the Holy City with his personal contingent of Teutonic knights and crowned himself the king of Jerusalem in the Church of the Holy Sepulchre the following day. He literally placed the crown on his own head, thus making himself even more infamous in the Holy Land. Frederick II was now not only the emperor of the Holy Roman Empire but also the king of Jerusalem. He returned to Acre, from where he hurried off to Europe, never to return to Outremer again.

Although the peculiar Sixth Crusade earned the excommunicated Emperor Frederick II a notorious reputation among the Latins, at least it managed to return the Holy City back into Christian hands (despite the German's suspicious means). Frederick's acquisition of territories without shedding Christian blood was indeed remarkable, and Outremer should have capitalized on it. After all, the Kingdom of Jerusalem was once again on its way to former glory. Instead, however, the Christian nobles continued having meaningless disputes among themselves, and the military orders followed them into chaos.

After Frederick left Outremer, no effort was made to consolidate the gains he had made, something that, somewhat logically, led to Jerusalem's capture in 1239 after the expiration of the truce. This, in turn, prompted yet another European expedition, namely the so-called Barons' Crusade, which was led by Theobald of Navarre, Richard of Cornwall, and Walter of Brienne. The crusaders relieved the pressure on Outremer, even managing to obtain control of the most land the Kingdom of Jerusalem had held after 1187 by the year 1241. Still, the Christians of Outremer would soon be confronted with the emergence of new hostile forces in the Levant.

The Khwarezmian Turks, who migrated west from central Asia, appeared in the Levant in the early 1240s. They were formidable horsemen and vicious fighters, and they mercilessly ran over the Middle East on their way to the Christian-held Holy Land by 1244, taking Tiberias and Nablus. The Latins were not prepared for this new foe and hurried to make preparations to defend Jerusalem. However, it was not enough. In June 1244, the city fell once again, and the ruthless Khwarezmians under Barka Khan murdered everybody they could get their hands on. Many Hospitaller knights, including the order's preceptor (commander of a preceptory), died fighting. The invaders set fire to the Church of the Holy Sepulchre and vandalized the holy relics that had been left untouched for hundreds of years by the conquerors of the city. It was the complete destruction of Jerusalem and everything for which it stood.

The Latins tried to retaliate, although they were nowhere near as strong as their foe. And if that was not enough, they got word that the Khwarezmians were about to join up with the Ayyubids in the south. The united effort of the enemy was guaranteed to eliminate Outremer in one swoop. Under Walter of Brienne, the Christians managed to gather about ten thousand troops to put up a final stand. Hospitaller Grand Master Guillaume de Chateauneuf and Templar Grand Master Armand de Perigord were also both there, commanding their respective knights. The Teutonic Knights were also represented on the battlefield. Interestingly, the Christians also had help from Muslim forces, which mainly came from Damascus, whose emir was in a succession dispute with the Ayyubids in Egypt. Together, the united force encountered the Ayyubid-Khwarezmian army, which had about the same number of men, northeast of Gaza in October 1244.

Confronted by the elite Turkish slave-soldiers of Egypt—the infamous Mamluks—the Christian force awaited orders. Walter of Brienne, who was perhaps reminded of the terrible deeds the Khwarezmians had done in Jerusalem, was adamant about engaging and ordered his men to set up in a fighting formation. The Muslim contingent made up the center-left flank of the army, while the military orders and the rest of the Franks took the right flank. The two armies engaged at La Forbie on October 17th in close fighting. During the course of the battle, the Khwarezmians managed to break the Damascene Muslims with a cavalry charge and split the Frankish army in two. It is not hard to guess what happened next. Outnumbered, the military orders and the knights of Outremer fought bravely to the bitter end. The Templar grand master and marshal were both slain in battle, while both Walter of Brienne and Hospitaller Grand Master Chateauneuf were taken as prisoners, along with hundreds of other soldiers. Out of the military orders, only about sixty Teutons, Templars, and Hospitallers survived in total. They fled to Ascalon. Thousands of men fell on the battlefield.

La Forbie was just as disastrous of a battle as Hattin had been nearly sixty years before.

The Fall of Outremer

Every Christian in the Holy Land realized that the end was near after La Forbie and that they could do almost nothing about it. Believing in the might of the military orders and with no other option to fight the much stronger enemy, Christian Outremer was painfully torn apart bit by bit. The threat of the Khwarezmians eventually faded, but the Egyptian Mamluks continued their assault on the Christian positions. The Mongol horde also appeared in the Levant in this period, putting pressure on the crusader holdings in the northern part of the Holy Land. In 1247, the Ayyubids marched on Ascalon, which was mainly defended by a small Hospitaller force. By October, the Christian attempts to reinforce the city from the sea had failed due to a storm that reduced their fleet to pieces. The Egyptians managed to take it relatively easily, slaughtering its garrison and everyone else that resisted the new conquerors.

In the months following the capture of Ascalon, yet another crusade would arrive in the Holy Land with the intention of relieving the pressure the Mongols and Mamluks had exerted on the Christians. Led by King Louis IX of France, the expedition arrived in the city of Limassol in Cyprus, where the crusaders discussed potential plans of action. Hospitaller Deputy Grand Master Jean de Ronay was present at the meeting and accompanied the crusaders to the battle. The objective was once again for the Egyptian coastal city of Damietta to gain access to the richest enemy lands.

At around the same time, the Hospitallers, who were acting on the orders of Pope Innocent IV, supposedly changed their uniforms. They adopted new red surcoats and blended them with the original black of their mantles, keeping the eight-pointed white cross. From the mid-13th century onward, the Hospitallers were depicted in chronicle records and popular paintings wearing their new uniforms.

As for the crusade, Louis IX waited the winter to sail to Damietta, doing so in the spring of 1249, engaging with the Egyptians on the coast. The Ayyubids retreated past Damietta, evacuating the city and allowing the crusaders to enter unopposed in early June. There, in the extreme heat of the Egyptian summer, the French king waited for his reinforcements, which eventually arrived in late autumn after being delayed by an overflooded Nile. In an ironic turn of events, where history repeated itself almost perfectly, the crusaders then embarked on a march to take Cairo. They found initial success at Mansurah in February of 1250. However, upon pushing farther, the Egyptian general Baibars (also spelled as Baybars) managed to outsmart the crusader army, which was already badly battered from the tiresome march up the Nile, as the men had suffered constant raids on their positions by the Muslim light cavalry. The Egyptians drew in the crusader vanguard, including hundreds of Templar knights, and launched a counter-offensive, eliminating some of the most professional soldiers of the crusader army. Only five Templars survived, including Grand Master Guillaume de Sonnac, who lost an eye. The French king's brother, Robert of Artois, was slain on the battlefield.

By early April, the crusaders were unable to make any more progress, and King Louis ordered a mass retreat to Damietta. However, the Egyptians were fighting in their homeland and knew how to maneuver their way around the Nile Delta better than the Christians. The Egyptians cut off their escape by opening the sluices, and much of the crusader army was relentlessly hunted down by the Muslims. King Louis was captured in the process, and Jean de Ronay fell on the battlefield. It was another terrible attempt at capturing Egypt, and it had produced nearly the same results as the attempt during the Fifth Crusade. About a thousand crusaders survived the expedition out of an initial force of about fifteen thousand men.

Louis IX was eventually ransomed and ended up in Acre, although he never came to terms with the disastrous defeat he had suffered at the hands of the Mamluks. He would return to France in 1254, ending the last major crusade without gaining anything for the Christians. As for the Hospitallers, they managed to get a better hand on the Assassin Order, imposing a yearly tribute on them. In fact, the Assassins had approached the Hospitallers since they needed men to defend their holdings against the Sunni Mongols who had come from the east. The connection between the Hospitallers and the Assassins persisted throughout the 13th century, although it is still probably an exaggeration to say the two had an amicable relationship. They had united because of their common rivals. Not only did they have the Mongols to contend with, but they also had the Templars to watch out for.

The Templar-Hospitaller rivalry persisted as Outremer shrunk in size from the Muslim incursions. It appeared that the two orders could not peacefully coexist unless they were together in a military campaign. As the Templars emerged as allies to Venice, the Hospitallers decided to naturally side with the Italian rivals of Venice, Genoa. Both Italian states had set up trade outposts in various cities in the Holy Land and pursued extensive trade with the help of the two orders. In their quarrels, which never stopped, even in Outremer, the Venetians and the Genoese managed to drag in the military orders, most infamously during an incident in 1256, known as the War of

Saint Sabas over an old monastery that separated the Genoese and the Venetian quarters of Acre. The monastery was claimed by both. Constant confrontations between the Italians in Acre eventually resulted in the two engaging in hand-to-hand combat in the streets of the city. Local nobility had bad blood with both Italian states and carefully chose their side. The military orders followed as well, leading to civic unrest that would last for years.

This was the first instant when the Templars and Hospitallers had resorted to actual fighting, although it was mostly contained in Acre since that was the point of contention between the Genoese and the Venetians. In the end, the military orders would be reconciled by Queen Plaisance of Cyprus, who personally sailed to Acre to see that the constant fighting had come to an end. Venice also got the upper hand in a naval confrontation, leading to the Genoese largely abandoning their interests in Acre. The War of Saint Sabas would persist for many years between the Italian states, although the Templars and Hospitallers would be preoccupied with more serious problems to actively participate. Still, this occurrence is a clear example of the divisions that existed between the two orders at the time when Christendom needed their unity the most.

Meanwhile, the Christian nobles were scrambling together whatever forces they had to confront the Egyptians under Sultan Baibars, who had personally participated in both victories over the crusaders in Egypt. The Latins even tried to ally with the Mongols, who had taken much of Anatolia and the eastern Levant by 1260, but this only made the sultan more determined to take them out. A constant series of attacks on Crusader territories began. Starting in 1263, Baibars clashed with the Christians on many occasions, taking their possessions one by one. He first marched on Acre but abandoned the siege, instead favoring to take Nazareth. After that, the sultan laid siege to the city of Arsuf, which had originally been taken by Richard the Lionheart. The city was garrisoned by a Hospitaller force of about 270 knights. The brothers held out in Arsuf for six weeks, repelling the attempts made by the Muslims to scale the walls and get into the city amidst the constant bombardment by their artillery. Still, their defense was not enough. The city eventually fell, and Baibars captured and executed all of the brothers who did not die during the siege.

This was followed by the capture of Templar-controlled Safad in July 1263. Just like in Arsuf, no Templar brothers were allowed to live. In the next two years, Baibars followed up his victories with the capture of Jaffa, Caesarea, Ascalon, and even Antioch, which was taken by the sultan in 1268. He reportedly defeated the city's large garrison, with his troops plundering Antioch and enslaving and massacring tens of thousands of its inhabitants.

The Hospitallers were confronted by Baibars in 1271 at their mighty Krak des Chevaliers. Out of the many castles in Outremer, Krak des Chevaliers was considered to have been one of the most magnificent, and no Muslim invader managed to take it after it had been entrusted to the order. As the Muslims approached the castle with their siege towers from the southern ridge, the only accessible point to the fortification, they were joined by the Assassins, who offered their help to the Egyptians against their tribute-masters. Despite the best efforts of the brothers, Baibars's men managed to open a breach in the southern walls, forcing the Hospitallers to retreat to the citadel, where they held out for another ten days. Baibars realized that the brothers would inflict many casualties on his force despite his numerical advantage, so he forged a letter from Grand Master Hugh de Revel, urging them to surrender the castle. The letter was delivered to the Hospitallers. Whether they believed it to have been the orders of their grand master or not, they probably realized their desperate situation and chose to abandon the castle, being promised safe passage from Baibars. In early April, as the Hospitallers fled Krak des Chevaliers, it was clear that the order's days were numbered.

Baibars passed away unexpectedly, and his successor, Qalawun, agreed to a temporary truce with the crusaders to direct their forces against the Mongols. However, at the Second Battle of Homs, which would be fought in 1281 between the Mongols and the Mamluks, Khan Mongke Temur would be joined by a Hospitaller contingent of about one hundred knights from the order's castle at Marqab. In the ensuing battle, their efforts would be rendered useless, as the Mamluks crushed the Mongol army, wounding their general. The rest of the Mongol forces retreated. This angered Qalawun, who blamed the Hospitallers for breaking the truce and started to plan his attack on perhaps the most formidable castle in all of Outremer and one of the last Hospitaller strongholds: Marqab.

Qalawun eventually attacked the castle in April 1285, employing numerous siege equipment and artillery. Marqab, which was conveniently located on a steep hill much like Krak des Chevaliers, was a tough fortification to take, giving the Hospitallers a natural defensive advantage. However, the brothers garrisoning the castle were severely outnumbered by the thousands of Mamluks at its gates. Still, for about five weeks, they defended it valiantly before Qalawun's engineers dug a secret tunnel that led to the north tower and blew it up from below, creating a breach in Marqab's defenses. Realizing that their position had been compromised, the Hospitallers offered to surrender. The Mamluks agreed, allowing the remaining brothers to leave the castle with whatever twenty-five mules could carry. Just like that, Marqab fell to the invaders. Qalawun wisely decided to repair its mighty walls instead of razing it to the ground, as he realized its strategic location.

The remaining Hospitallers fled to Tripoli, one of the only Christian enclaves in northern Syria. The Latins knew their days were numbered and offered King Henry II of Cyprus, a descendant of Guy de Lusignan, to come to Acre and lead them in battle. Although the latter arrived in Tyre in 1286 and was greeted enthusiastically by the public, he only managed to create a fake sense of unity among the remaining dwellers of Outremer before sailing back to his island.

Meanwhile, Qalawun continued his rampage along the Palestine coast, taking port after port. In March of 1289, he assembled his forces and marched on Tripoli, where Countess Lucia of Tripoli tried to put up a last stand with whatever men she had at her disposal. Hospitaller Marshal Matthew de Clermont and Templar Marshal Geoffrey de Vandac were both present in the city, although they commanded no more than three hundred knights in total. The exact number of attackers or the men in the garrison is unknown, but it is safe to estimate that Qalawun's army far outnumbered the defenders, and that is what ultimately made the difference. As the city's walls crumbled from the large rocks hurled at them by the Muslim catapults, Countess Lucia, along with other important figures like the two marshals, managed to flee Tripoli. Qalawun decimated the city's population, ending about 180 years of uninterrupted Christian rule of the city. He razed the city to the ground and proceeded to turn his attention to Acre, the last of the crusader strongholds in Outremer.

Although Qalawun died before getting to Acre, his successor, al-Ashraf Khalil, successfully continued his father's legacy, leading his army to the Christian city in early April 1291. Sources suggest that the Muslim army counted about 100,000 men in total, while the total garrison in Acre did not exceed 15,000 men at best. Almost all of the remaining influential Christians assembled in the city, hoping that its large walls could withstand the barrage of Mamluk catapults and mangonels. All three military orders were present with whatever men they had, including the Hospitaller Grand Master Jean de Villiers and Marshal Matthew de Clermont. Amalric of Tyre, Henry II's brother, was nominally in charge of the city's overall defenses.

The bombardment began on April 6th when the Mamluks opened fire on the defenders. For almost ten days, the defenders endured the Muslim barrage, but on the night of April 15th, some Templar brothers sallied out to unexpectedly attack the Muslim camp, but to no avail. The Hospitallers tried a similar tactic a couple of nights later, but by then, the Muslims were better prepared and killed every brother in combat. About a month after the beginning of the siege, King Henry of Cyprus sent reinforcements consisting of about two thousand infantrymen with ships, which joined the city's defenses from the port. Still, by mid-May, the Muslims were closing in, having breached several points along the city walls. On May 16th, they stormed St. Anthony's Gate but were repelled, thanks to brave fighting from the defending Templars and Hospitallers. Then, the invaders focused their attention on the least defended portion of the city, the so-called Accursed Tower, managing to take it down and creating more weaknesses in the defense. By this point, the Muslims had already occupied some outer parts of the city, forcing the defenders to fall back.

Gradually, the defenders started to flee on their ships. The only destination they could go to was the island of Cyprus. Utilizing the Venetian and Genoese galleys in the port, as well as the ships on which King Henry's men had arrived, the city's inhabitants flocked to the port, trying to get out as the Muslims closed in. Thousands were left behind in the chaos, including children who were abandoned by their parents who wanted to save their skins. Patriarch Nicholas of Hanapes drowned while on his boat because it was too overcrowded and collapsed. Despite the best efforts of the military orders that stayed behind to fight the Muslims, only a minority of the city's population managed to survive. An estimated sixty thousand people were either enslaved or outright massacred by the Mamluks.

The fall of Acre was followed by the fall of the remaining castles of Outremer in the next months. It was the death of the Christians in the Holy Land after almost two centuries of struggling for survival. The few brothers of the Knights Hospitaller and the rest of the city's people who managed to flee would eventually end up in Cyprus. There, the Hospitallers would start a new chapter in the order's history.

Chapter Six – Hospitaller Rhodes

Knights Hospitaller in Cyprus

The fall of Outremer certainly came as a shock to Christendom, which mourned the loss of the Holy Land to the Muslim heathens. The three military orders, or whatever was left of them, continued their existence, albeit very differently from each other. The eighty or so Hospitallers, headed by Grand Master Jean de Villiers, decided to stay at Limassol for a while under the protection of King Henry II.

The Hospitallers offered the king their services while grieving the loss of Outremer, although they hoped to someday return to it. The Teutons gave up on the Holy Land altogether, finding refuge in the German lands of central Europe and making Marienburg their headquarters, after which they eventually settled along the Baltic and emerged as influential regional actors in northeast Europe. The Templars, on the other hand, the wealthiest and the most powerful of the three, flocked to their numerous castles in Europe, settling mainly in France. They continued their existence in relative comfort.

With the loss of Outremer, it was clear that the general attitude toward the religious military orders was changing drastically, with the European lords no longer valuing the services they provided to them. After all, they had failed their main mission of defending the Holy Land. Why should they be trusted?

Still, surprisingly, out of the three, the Knights Templar would feel the harsh consequences of the changing times the most. Despite losing their possessions in Outremer, the Templars were still one of the most influential forces in France. They enjoyed the security and independence granted to them by the papacy and managed to more than adequately sustain themselves financially due to the merits of their numerous businesses and the gracious donations they had received in the past. In fact, their influence had grown to the extent that they were almost running a small state of their own, which was one of the contributing factors to their rapid decline. In 1310, Philip IV of France ordered the arrest of all Templars, charging them with blasphemy, conspiracy, satanism, and heretical behavior of the worst kind. Whether or not these charges against the Templars were true, the French king probably wanted to get rid of the order to avoid it being a nuisance in the future.

In the following months, the Templar brothers were condemned in public trials and executed throughout France. Pope Clement V, who was under the influence of the French king, officially abolished the order in 1312. This abrupt ending of the Knights Templar is shrouded in mystery to this day.

Templar possessions in France were officially transferred to the Hospitallers, and the rest of the Templars who managed to evade the arrests gradually went underground, stopping their activities in Europe. However, the Hospitallers were in no position to maintain all of the Templar holdings because they had no manpower or funds of their own. They also believed they would one day go back to Outremer and continue their noble mission of fighting in the name of Christ. In fact, the order tried to maintain its close relationship with the papacy. When the Templars were still around in the first years of the 1300s, there were even talks of organizing a joint Templar-Hospitaller-led crusade to reclaim the Holy Land. Hospitaller Grand Master Foulques de Villaret, who was elected in 1305, proposed the idea of launching a series of naval raids on the Muslim-held coastline of Outremer to soften up their positions and strike decisively when the enemy was weak.

However, his plans were flawed and superficial, relying on support from a very weak Cilician Armenia and the newly Islamified Mongols, which was unlikely to happen. In addition, Europe was largely done with expeditions to Outremer, as the once strong crusading fervor had almost completely disappeared. The royal houses of England and France were engaged in a struggle with each other, the Holy Roman Empire was unstable and without an emperor, the Iberians were still in the middle of the Reconquista, and the Italian states were bickering among themselves, trying to gain influence in the Mediterranean. In short, no one was willing to go on another crusade, and the Hospitaller grand master's proposal was eventually denied.

Instead, what the order preoccupied itself with was rebuilding and reorganization, still hoping that the idea of returning to Outremer was not too unrealistic. There was little to do with less than a hundred men, and despite the training the brothers underwent, it was difficult to maintain the same standards of discipline as during the heyday of the order in the Holy Land. The Hospitallers settled at the Saint Hilarion fortress located on a mountaintop, which they started to rebuild. There were many fortifications in Cyprus, which were built mainly to repel naval attempts to take the island, so the Hospitallers probably helped in keeping them maintained with the expertise they had accumulated during their years in Outremer. After their move to Cyprus, the office of the admiral was officially created since the order came in possession of a small flotilla to patrol the coast.

Ultimately, however, the Hospitallers' stay in Cyprus was destined to be a short one from the very beginning, not least because their hopes were high of going back to Outremer. The island was never truly perceived as a permanent settlement, and the lack of discipline that came with inactivity, as well as the general change in attitude toward the military orders after the fall of Outremer, slowly put the Hospitallers at odds with King Henry II, who, much like, Philip IV of France, believed that he would be better off without the order in his kingdom. Not only were the Hospitallers fully independent, but they were also devout Roman Catholics on a small island whose population was mostly Greek Orthodox, something that also contributed to their disagreements with the locals and the king. In addition, new recruits who joined the organization in Cyprus were no longer members of the nobility of Europe coming to fight for the good of Christendom. Instead, most of them were low-born with no real fighting experience and were not as pious as average brothers. Still, the order accepted them to their ranks because it needed more men. Gradually, the overall religious aspect of the order would decline, and the Hospitallers would become more warriors than monks.

After much consideration, the Greek island of Rhodes was chosen by the order as a potential place to resettle, as the situation with King Henry was getting tenser. Rhodes was under the jurisdiction of the Byzantine Empire, although once-great Byzantium was slowly being squeezed out of its former territories in Anatolia by the Ottoman Turks, the latter of which was a new rising power. By the mid-1300s, Rhodes was virtually an independent island, with Constantinople having no real control over it.

Located in the southeastern part of the Aegean Sea, it was one of the largest islands in the area. It was mostly subject to Italian merchant influences, who had established it as a sort of trade colony, much like the former Greek islands. Grand Master Foulques de Villaret reportedly engaged in talks over the possession of the island with a Genoese lord of the island, Vignolo de' Vignoli, in 1306. However, Vignoli was not technically fully in charge of the island, so the deal that was struck between the two probably amounted to the shared possession of Rhodes, with its different castles and neighboring islands mostly falling under the administration of the grand master.

Whatever the case, it would take the Hospitallers the next three years to consolidate their hold on the island. This period included several armed confrontations with the locals, as well as outside forces who had claims on the island. The Knights Hospitaller probably launched an invasion of its own and came to conquer the island by force in 1310, fighting the Italians and Byzantine forces on their way.

Moving to Rhodes

After a small interlude following the fall of Outremer, during which time the Knights Hospitaller spent at Cyprus, the order fully relocated to Rhodes by 1310. Much like they had done previously, they spent the first few years at their new home adapting and reorganizing the order's administration. To solidify their position as the new masters of the island, the Hospitallers had to do quite a lot, including defending the territories from Turkish attacks and assimilating themselves with the local Greek Orthodox population of Rhodes. In addition, they had to maintain close relationships with the pope and the rest of the Catholics in the area to gain their support against the Turks, who were slowly expanding in size at the expense of the ailing Byzantines.

A new addition to the order's structure was the introduction of the offices of the "tongues" (*linguae*). As the name suggests, this new layer of bureaucracy meant the division of the Hospitallers into distinct groups based on the brothers' ethnolinguistic background. By this time, the Knights Hospitaller was an organization with members from all over Europe, so it made sense that they would be divided into different groups based on their origin, with a dedicated leader assigned to each group. This was also reflected when it came to governing the order's overseas possessions. Other lower-level ranks were also introduced to make administrating more coherent. There were seven tongues in total in France, Auvergne, Provence, Germany, England, Italy, and Aragon. Although not all the roles and distinctions were finalized at the beginning, the system would eventually be fleshed out to allow for a smoother running of the order.

Despite the fact that the Hospitaller Order had managed to successfully take the island (or buy it), financially speaking, the Hospitallers were nowhere near their former glory. They had to rebuild their wealth basically from scratch, engaging in many different activities to do so, like banking (much like their Templars brothers, although on a much smaller scale). They also started to cultivate sugar and wine plantations on the island. A lot of the order's wealth came from overseas, as the different regional *linguae* sent a portion of their revenue to Rhodes. Other sources of income included donations, booty the Hospitallers obtained from their occasional raids on the Turks, and legal or trade services they offered to the passing Christians.

Throughout all this time, the order maintained good relations with the pope, and the extent of the connections between the two would be demonstrated throughout the 14th century on many different occasions. For example, in the year 1317, the Hospitaller brethren grew wary of Grand Master Foulques de Villaret, who was accused of being too ambitious. Indeed, the grand master was adamant about building up the fortifications in Rhodes and expanding the order's possessions on smaller Aegean islands. These were very costly endeavors, especially since the Hospitallers lacked manpower. The brothers were fed up with the almost despotic manner in which de Villaret administered the order, and they tried to depose him in 1317, forcing him to flee to the Hospitaller castle of Lindos located on

Rhodes.

The upset brothers elected a new interim leader and tried to arrest the grand master, but thanks to the efforts of Pope John XXII, the two sides would be reconciled and agreed to a compromise. The pope summoned the leading brothers to his residence in Auvergne, with de Villaret being among them. The pope proposed Helion de Villeneuve as the new grand master. The proposal was eventually accepted, and de Villeneuve was officially elected in 1319.

Helion de Villeneuve would prove to be a wise leader, and during his time in power, the order would be mostly preoccupied with consolidating its position in the region. The Hospitallers came into possession of the neighboring islands of Karpathos, Kasos, and Kos in the early 1310s, and significant resources were devoted to building safe fortifications in these new acquisitions to defend against the Ottoman Turks. Utilizing the knowledge they had gained while manning the magnificent castles in Outremer, the Hospitallers proceeded to construct new strongholds or build upon the existing castles that had been built by the Byzantines. The main castle in the city of Rhodes was, of course, the most formidable of the new constructions. Each new stronghold was designed to hold a garrison of about 1,500 soldiers, although the order did not have enough members at the time to fully meet this number at every place. Over the next few decades, further efforts from the following grand masters contributed to the building of about twenty or so new fortifications in Hospitaller-owned lands.

Thanks to their good relations with the papacy, the Hospitallers were able to ameliorate their relations with France, Venice, and Cyprus, entering into a sort of defensive alliance with these Catholic nations in the 1330s. This closeness manifested during the so-called Smyrniote crusades, which were called by Pope Clement VI on the Turkish-controlled city of Smyrna in Western Anatolia in 1343. The Catholics joined forces and managed to successfully capture the strategically placed ancient city, with the Hospitallers playing a key role. Just like in many previous instances, they brought professionalism and discipline to the crusader army, which was mainly commanded by Hugh IV of Cyprus. Taking the castle in Smyrna from the Turks was very important to maintain firm control of the Aegean, where the Ottomans colluded with pirates to undermine Christian naval power. The crusaders would hold onto the city for the next half a century.

The capture of Smyrna provided the Hospitallers with even more opportunities to increase their competence at sea, and the order's naval capabilities exponentially improved after settling at Rhodes. The Hospitallers came into the possession of dozens of galleys and smaller ships they could maneuver in the tight and shallow waters of the Aegean. The Hospitallers became a real force to be reckoned with, managing to confront the Turks at sea on several occasions. With the experiences they accumulated from constant engagements with the enemy, the natural need for naval expertise due to being situated on an island, and their close contact with the Venetians, the Hospitallers managed to improve their shipbuilding and naval tactics. This was proven during a naval engagement at Imbros in 1347, where a combined Venetian-Hospitaller flotilla managed to decisively defeat the Ottoman corsairs.

This and many other smaller victories against the Muslims were followed up with another impressive occurrence: the so-called Alexandrian Crusade in 1365, where the Christians landed in the Egyptian city of Alexandria. After a long siege, they emerged victorious. The crusaders, who were enthusiastic about the success at Smyrna, wanted to face new challenges, and the growing naval power of the Hospitallers and the Venetians certainly persuaded them to try attacking Alexandria. The Christians smashed the Egyptian fleet off the coast and proceeded to enter the city before deciding that sacking it was the best option. This expedition was one of the most successful of the Crusades we have covered in this book.

In 1377, Juan Fernandez de Heredia, an Aragonese knight of noble descent, became the Hospitaller Order's thirty-first grand master. The new grand master's tenure coincided with the period of the Papal Schism of the late 1370s, which saw the election of two popes, one of whom resided in Rome and the other in the French town of Avignon. (The schism had been a product of decades of instability in the papacy, which had been constantly influenced by the French Crown since the early 14th century.) In fact, de Heredia helped Pope Gregory XI build fortifications at Avignon, for which the pope repaid him by appointing him as the grand master, something he technically had no authority to do since the brothers always elected a grand master from their own.

In 1383, the situation would be complicated even more when the rival pope, Urban VI, who resided in Rome, sacked de Heredia, instead appointing the Italian Riccardo Caracciolo in his place, who would be referred to as the "anti-master" during his twelve-year tenure. The Italian would never gain enough support from the order, with de Heredia continuing to largely be regarded as the leader until his death in 1396. The Hospitallers elected Philibert de Nailac as his replacement, ending the confusion. We shall not go into great detail about the Papal Schism and the Hospitallers' involvement in it, but the incident indicates how closely the order was tied to the developments in the papacy—a relationship that was sometimes uncomfortable for the Hospitallers.

Philibert de Nailac would kick off his time in the office of the grand master by leading his fellow knights into yet another crusade. This one was called because of the ever-growing expansion of the Ottoman Empire into the Balkans. In fact, the Turks had made their way deep into eastern Europe, having subjugated most of the Byzantine territories and smaller independent Christian nations. This alarmed King Sigismund III of Hungary. He clashed with the Ottomans many times throughout his life. He desperately sought help from the West, looking to reignite the spirit of the golden days of the Crusades. Sigismund III would lead a huge army of about 100,000 men in total. The army was comprised of some sixty thousand Hungarians, six thousand Germans, ten thousand French, ten thousand Wallachians, and about fifteen thousand soldiers from other parts of Europe, including a contingent of the Knights Hospitaller. The crusaders started their march in mid-1396 from Budapest and targeted the city of Nicopolis on the Danube, which was a very important location they knew was not adequately defended.

However, the mighty army of King Sigismund was plagued by an array of problems. Overzealous with the infamous crusading spirit, the soldiers started pillaging innocent villages on their way to Nicopolis, failing to maintain the discipline that was needed for a cohesive campaign. Once they approached their target, they were surprised to find an Ottoman relief force commanded by Sultan Bayezid I. The men prepared for battle in late September. In the chaotic battle that ensued, thousands of crusaders defied the orders of the king. The

Ottomans emerged victorious, crushing the Christian army and capturing thousands. King Sigismund, alongside the Hospitaller grand master, would manage to somehow escape by the river. Philibert of Nailac would never forget the shameful defeat at Nicopolis and the might of the Ottoman sword.

Thus, it is logical that upon his return to Rhodes, fortifying the island truly took off. The brothers consulted with Italian and Greek master artisans and completed the work on many defensive walls and towers, not only in more urban areas but also along the coasts, to watch for potential Turkish invasions. The Hospitallers transformed the landscape of the island and made Rhodes one of the most well-defended places in Europe. The great castles built by the order still stand today, attracting many curious visitors. Due to their longevity, they have become the most recognizable part of the Hospitallers' legacy.

The Fall of Rhodes

The next 150 years after the Crusade of Nicopolis would be the period when the Knights Hospitaller would see the most action since leaving Outremer. By then, the military order controlled several smaller islands in the Aegean alongside Rhodes, as well as the castles in Smyrna and Bodrum on the Anatolian Peninsula, the latter being rebuilt and fortified from the ruins of the ancient Greek site of Halicarnassus. The fortifications at the main stronghold of Rhodes were also built up to help defend the order's headquarters from a potential Turkish invasion, the threat of which always hung in the air. Different tongues of the order were assigned garrisoning and maintenance duties of the large walls of Rhodes to make its potential defense easier and more cohesive. In the late 14th century, the order also constructed the Palace of the Grand Master and modernized the towers to accommodate the order's new guns and cannons.

In December 1402, the Hospitallers were approached at their castle in Smyrna by a new Asiatic conqueror who had managed to sweep through his opposition like his central Asian predecessors before him. Timur, the infamous, ruthless, but nevertheless brilliant general with Mongol origins, posed a great threat to Ottoman power in Anatolia, defeating Sultan Bayezid I at Ankara. Smyrna was only manned by about two hundred or so knights at the time, and the brothers were confident they would hold out, despite the Timurids' sheer numbers. The castle was bordered by the sea on one side and a deep ditch on the other, which separated it from the rest of the Anatolian Plateau, offering a natural barrier to any invaders. Despite the Hospitallers' high hopes, they were probably not expecting the scale of the Timurid bombardment that was about to descend upon their walls. Heavy fire from blazing rocks, mangonels, catapults, and cannons forced the brothers to give up once Smyrna's walls started to crumble. The Hospitallers managed to get on ships and abandoned the castle, fleeing to Bodrum, which was about one hundred miles to the south.

Timur would pass away soon after his attack on Smyrna, giving the Ottomans time to reconsolidate their hold on Anatolia and eastern Europe. However, Ottoman Sultan Mehmed II had no time to address the Hospitaller problem on Rhodes since he was busy taking Constantinople in May 1453, putting an end to the thousand-year history of the Byzantine Empire. The Hospitaller galleys had become a real thorn in the side of the Ottomans in the Aegean, with the brothers constantly disrupting the naval activities of the Turks, which allowed the Christians to control the seas. Through their relationship with Venice, the Hospitallers were able to expand the reach of their naval power into the South Mediterranean, something that annoyed the Egyptian Mamluks, who even launched a campaign against the Hospitallers at Rhodes, besieging the city in 1444. Thanks to the efforts of Grand Master Jean de Lastic, the Hospitallers easily repelled the disorganized Mamluk expedition, reclaiming some of the smaller settlements on the island that had fallen to the Egyptians. It seemed that as long as the Hospitallers fought in the safety of their mighty fortifications, betting against them was never a wise choice. For this reason, in the years following the siege in 1444, many inhabitants of less-protected Hospitaller-controlled islands were relocated to Rhodes.

In the 1460s, the order was briefly involved in the succession dispute of the Kingdom of Cyprus. The Hospitallers supported Charlotte, the daughter of the recently deceased King John III. The military order actually clashed with the Venetians, who backed the illegitimate son of the king, James. At the time, the two were the biggest naval powers in the eastern part of the Mediterranean, and although they united against the Ottomans, they sometimes had conflicting interests and ambitions to overtake each other.

The struggle with Venice did not prove to be a wise move for the order, as the confrontations with the Venetians dried up the Hospitallers' coffers. In the mid-1460s, the conflict was resolved through negotiations. To make up for the financial crisis, the order's grand master, Piero Raimondo Zacosta, introduced a small tax on the arriving merchant ships at Rhodes.

In 1479, the island of Rhodes once again came under threat, this time by the Ottomans, who landed a relatively small-scale reconnaissance mission under Ishak Pasha and began pillaging the settlements. The Hospitallers had utilized the time after their dispute with Venice to build up their island's defenses even more, so they were able to defeat the intruders, forcing them to fall back. However, Ishak Pasha returned to Rhodes about a year later with a much larger force with the aim of taking the island. It seemed that he had assessed the situation during his previous visit and believed that he could take Rhodes for the sultan. Thus, in May of 1480, he landed his 20,000 or so men south of the city of Rhodes, with the 170 ships that carried the army anchored just offshore. It seemed that the Hospitallers were about to withstand a real test on their beloved castle.

Grand Master Pierre d'Aubusson, a capable veteran knight who was fifty-seven years old, organized the castle's defense with a garrison of about 2,500. The men watched from the walls as the enemy siege towers, cannons, rams, and mortars were rolled up close to the city. Pierre d'Aubusson denied Ishak Pasha's request for surrender, after which the Ottoman commander started the bombardment of the city.

The Ottomans' main objective appears to have been the menacing Saint Nicholas Tower, which looked over the port on the northern wall. It took about a week of bombardment and over three hundred cannonballs to crack the tower, whose defenders, led by the Italian knight Fabrizio del Carretto, kept repairing the holes made by the cannons with the debris. They even utilized the help of local civilians to put up artificial defenses in place of the tower.

In June, Ishak Pasha decided to storm the position, covering his forces with cannon fire as they breached the walls, but the defenders were still going strong. They met the Ottoman soldiers with fire pots and hot oil, which they poured down from the walls, burning the attackers and lowering their morale. From the gaps in the walls, they rained down their arrows and crossbow bolts until the Ottomans had to abandon their charge.

Fabrizio del Carretto and his knights withstood two more offensives on their position at Saint Nicholas Tower even when a part of the wall was opened up, and the city's Jewish quarter (located in a nearby area) was forced to evacuate to the center. Grand Master d'Aubusson, meanwhile, ordered their houses to be razed to the ground to make it more difficult for the attackers to pass through, with the knights even putting down traps and barricades. Ishak Pasha tried to land some of his men along the other sections of the wall, but the French Tongue repelled the disorganized attackers with arrow fire. Eventually, in late June, the defenders managed to set ablaze several of the Ottoman ships from the trebuchet they had built inside the city that fired over the walls. The grand master even personally joined the Italian Tongue in defending the breach at Saint Nicholas Tower, suffering four wounds but continuing to fight until a final thrust in the chest penetrated his armor and damaged his lung. He was then carried out of the battle.

Yet, the Hospitallers managed to hold out until August, and once they saw that the enemy's spirit was no longer high, they charged and brought the fight to the Ottoman camp. All of the tongues joined for a combined assault, killing about three thousand enemies in their counter-attack and forcing Ishak Pasha to flee. With Ottoman heads on their spikes, they returned to the city, victorious, praising the Lord and their grand master, who managed to survive a very dangerous wound and continued to exercise his duties for the next twenty-three years. The defense of Rhodes in 1480 was one of the Hospitallers' most remarkable military feats, proving once again that, when operating wisely and cohesively, the order was one of the most dangerous forces to be reckoned with.

Still, the Ottoman threat was by no means neutralized, and the Hospitallers set about rebuilding their best-defended castle at Rhodes. The city needed extensive repairs, as the northern section of the wall was heavily damaged, including Saint Nicholas Tower and the Palace of the Grand Master. A strong earthquake in 1481 did even more damage to the city's structures, making it more difficult for the knights to repair the fortifications. But with the help of the locals, who had increasingly flocked into the city, afraid of Ottoman attacks on their villages, Rhodes was gradually built up.

However, all good things must come to an end, and that included the Hospitallers' time at Rhodes. More than forty years after Ishak Pasha's attempt, Sultan Suleyman (Suleiman) the Magnificent, largely regarded as the most accomplished Ottoman sultan in history, would march on the order's headquarters with the biggest army the Ottomans had specifically assembled to deal with the Hospitallers. The sultan notoriously disliked the Hospitallers, regarding them as Christian pirates in the Aegean. He was fed up with the constant disruption the brothers had brought upon his people. In June 1522, about four thousand Ottoman galleys approached the coast of the island, carrying an estimated eighty thousand soldiers and dropping them off at Kallithea Bay, ten miles south of the port of Rhodes. Medieval chroniclers mention that the Ottoman force was 200,000 strong, although that is highly unlikely and probably an exaggeration. Mustafa Pasha led the Turks at first, but about a month after their arrival in Rhodes, Sultan Suleyman personally took charge, arriving in late July.

What could the Hospitallers do against such a mighty force? It seems they were aware the Ottomans were planning another offensive on their headquarters and bolstered the defenses on the island to make the siege as difficult as possible for their enemy. Fabrizio del Carretto, who had distinguished himself during the siege of 1480 and was eventually elected as the order's forty-second grand master, was responsible for setting up additional defenses along the city walls. He passed away a year before the Ottomans launched their offensive, but the order was still under the leadership of a very wise man, Philippe Villiers de L'Isle-Adam, who asked the Europeans to send help to relieve the order at Rhodes before the siege began. However, the Europeans were engulfed in endless political struggles among themselves and did not respond, leaving the grand master and his seven thousand or so men to their own devices.

The main brunt of the assault was born by the English and Spanish Tongues of the order, which were stationed at the northeastern portion of the wall. The brothers could only watch as sixty mighty Ottoman cannons relentlessly shelled their positions for days. The defenders answered with artillery of their own, but the volume of their fire was nowhere near what the attackers had on the field. However, despite the sheer scale of the bombardment, it was not the sultan's main strategy, as he knew the strength of the walls. He employed thousands of experienced miners and sappers, whom he tasked with digging tunnels under the city walls and placing mines to blow them up from below. This tactic was not a new one in medieval warfare, although the sultan decided to implement it on a never-before-seen scale.

To counter this, a Hospitaller engineer, Gabriele Tadini da Martinengo, devised his own strategy. He placed drums on the inner side of the walls and attached chains to them, which he connected to the ground. Any vibration from below would be instantly detected by the garrison, thanks to the sound of the bells. Of course, this method was by no means perfect, but the brothers were able to detect the approximate location of several tunnels and took measures to avoid collateral damage from the enemy mines.

Despite the Hospitallers' numerical disadvantage, they withstood the siege valiantly for months, fighting off the occasional swarms of enemies that tried to breach the walls. The first real challenge and extensive hand-to-hand combat enveloped on September 4th, when a large portion of the wall at the English sector was blown up by the Ottomans. Suleyman ordered his men to flock into the ten-mile-wide gap, but he was disappointed to find that the defending English knights managed to kill about two thousand of his men at the breach. The knights held the walls and forced the enemy to fall back.

In late September, the Ottomans attempted another large-scale assault on the Hospitaller positions, this time firing so-called "dirty gunpowder" from their cannons, which produced thick smoke in the air, making it difficult for the defenders to see. After the visibility of the Hospitallers was severely limited, thousands of Ottomans charged on September 24th. Repelling this advance required a combined effort of all of the Tongues. Grand Master de L'Isle-Adam fought alongside his brothers personally. After six hours of vicious fighting, the Hospitallers were somehow still standing, having killed ten to fifteen thousand Ottomans in a single charge and having lost more than three hundred knights themselves.

Throughout October, the Turks launched several more head-on assaults on the Hospitaller positions, but the brothers managed to repulse every one of them. Still, by November, it was becoming clear the Hospitallers had exhausted their defenses, and the constant fighting had cost them a large portion of their standing garrison. The city's population had also been living in terrible conditions for months, as the people were under constant fire from the enemy artillery and on the brink of starvation. Surrender had never been an option for the brothers, as they knew the attackers were also pretty badly battered from all their unsuccessful attempts of breaking through. Perhaps the order's grand master hoped they would soon be dissuaded from continuing the siege.

As for Suleyman, the sultan had grown impatient with the siege but was amazed by the Hospitallers' bravery. He had lost many men in the siege against a much smaller enemy and wanted to deal with the Hospitallers as soon as possible. Realizing that he had to appeal to the people of Rhodes, the sultan ordered his men to fire arrows with attached pieces of paper that promised safety to the citizens if they surrendered or a painful death if Rhodes continued to put up a fight. Suleyman knew there was no other way the Hospitallers would give up their precious castle.

Ultimately, this approach worked. The city's inhabitants, who probably could have held out, naïvely believed the Ottoman sultan. Exhausted from the siege, they asked Grand Master de L'Isle-Adam to surrender to save their lives. Suleyman stopped the bombardment for a few days so the people of Rhodes could consider the proposal. At first, the grand master hesitated and delayed his answer, after which the Ottomans were ordered to continue the siege with extra effort. As new cracks appeared in the walls and as the defending brothers were slowly overwhelmed by the never-ending swarms of enemy forces, a white flag was finally waved by the Hospitallers in late December, signaling their surrender. On December 22nd, the grand master and his companion knights negotiated the terms with the sultan while four hundred or so Turkish Janissary troops marched into the city center unopposed.

Thus, on January 1st, 1523, the Knights Hospitaller evacuated the great city of Rhodes, a formidable fortification that had served as the order's headquarters for over two centuries. Grand Master de L'Isle-Adam left Rhodes with no more than two hundred of his fellow knights, accompanied by several thousand Christian inhabitants of the city, who carried with them whatever valuables they could. The people boarded the order's ships and sailed away from their homes, tragically concluding yet another chapter for the Knights Hospitaller.

Chapter Seven – Hospitaller Malta

Searching for a New Home

The Hospitallers' expulsion from Rhodes shocked the order. Much like in 1291 when they were forced out of Outremer, the Hospitallers were presented with a serious challenge. They needed to find a new place to move their headquarters. The Hospitallers virtually had no money or members. Grand Master Phillipe Villiers de L'Isle-Adam at first had set his eyes on the nearby island of Crete, then held by the Venetians. But the idea was scrapped since Venice was fighting a losing war against the Ottomans, who were slowly replacing them as masters of the Mediterranean. Disappointed and desperate, the grand master thus decided to head to Italy in hopes of finding a permanent residence there with the help of his most trusted ally, the pope.

The Hospitallers arrived in Italy in early 1523 and were offered by Pope Adrian VI to set up their new headquarters at Viterbo, located north of Rome. For his efforts, Grand Master de L'Isle-Adam was named "Defender of the Faith" by the pope. Of course, the order accepted this proposal, although the Hospitallers only spent four years at their new headquarters before being forced to move again in 1527. Throughout these four years, the order lived modestly, with few new recruits. They essentially returned to their wholesome beginnings. The Hospitallers had lost almost all their might and were in no shape to continue fighting for Christendom.

In 1527, Rome was sacked by Holy Roman Emperor Charles V, a member of the famous Habsburg dynasty and undoubtedly the most powerful man in Europe at the time. He controlled not only the German lands of the Holy Roman Empire but also parts of Italy and Spain. Traditionally, the emperor had a long-standing feud with the papacy, something that was only amplified by the ongoing Protestant Reformation, which drastically turned the tide of Christianity in Europe.

When Charles V sacked the ancient city with thirty thousand men, the Hospitallers came to the realization that the pope was no longer strong enough to be able to defend the order. The Hospitallers were forced to watch the Lutheran Germans spend many months in the city. Charles V never converted to Protestantism, although waging war against the pope certainly was not a good look for him. He was aware of the military orders' past tendencies to exercise uncontrollable independence if given the opportunity, so after dealing with His Holiness, he approached the Knights Hospitaller and offered them a new permanent place of dwelling: the island of Malta.

The proposal seemed logical. The order was already accustomed to living on an island, and Malta, located just south of Sicily, was a suitable place to be run by the Hospitallers. They could lend a hand in thwarting the domination of the Mediterranean by the Ottomans. The only thing Charles asked was for the order to annually send a Maltese falcon as a gift to the viceroy of Sicily, who was under the jurisdiction of the Holy Roman emperor.

The grand master accepted the offer, and in 1530, eight years after being forced out of Rhodes, the order finally moved to Malta. However, to put it mildly, Malta was a very obvious downgrade from Rhodes. It was neither as rich in soil nor as big as Rhodes, and the Maltese population was not keen on the arrival of the Hospitallers. Nevertheless, the order got to work, setting up its headquarters at the port city of Birgu. They slowly but surely built up the island and its harbors. Fort St. Angelo, which was built on ancient Roman ruins in Birgu, became one of the most eye-catching structures the order ever built. It withstood the test of time due to its defensive attributes and still stands proudly in Birgu as a proud testament to the Hospitallers' legacy.

Although the order still sought to maintain its crusading spirit against the infidel Muslims who occupied North Africa and eyed Malta, the Hospitallers had to adapt to the new times in which they lived. Christendom was in a crisis, being torn apart by the Protestant Reformation, and the European powers were extensively warring with each other to establish a new world order. In addition, the 16th century was the beginning of the Age of Discovery, with the newly discovered New World attracting more and more interested explorers from Europe. Amidst all of this, no one really had time to think about the old-fashioned idea of the Crusades, especially as the pope's role was being undermined. Sultan Suleyman, the most powerful Muslim in the world, even found an unlikely strategic ally in France's Francis I, as both of them were keen on the fall of Charles V's realm in central-eastern Europe.

Thus, the Knights Hospitaller, from the mid-16th century onward, would see its role as a Christian military order slowly diminish. Instead, as the order continued to rebuild its status and make Malta its new home, it slowly transformed into a political player more oriented toward establishing naval power in the Mediterranean. In the coming centuries, this transformation materialized when the Hospitaller Order came into possession of some islands in the Caribbean, embracing the age of exploration. However, before the order entered its period of decline, one development would shape its legacy forever, underlining once again that despite tough times, the Hospitallers always managed to maintain their fighting prowess and spirit.

The Great Siege

For the first twenty years after relocating to Malta, the Hospitallers tried to return back to their glory days and participated, with whatever men they had, in the campaigns of several European rulers. They slowly built up the island to the standards to which they were accustomed, securing it just enough to allow them to commit to expeditions. The navy was also improved, and the order became a reliable naval patrol against the Muslim pirates who lurked in the Mediterranean. The Hospitallers forged good relations with the Europeans, who helped the order replenish its ranks with fresh recruits, especially from the Catholic lands of Spain, Portugal, and Italy, which was different from the previous make-up of the order, which was once mostly comprised of French and German volunteers.

Thanks to this active involvement, the order would come to garrison the castle of Tripoli in North Africa, signaling to their enemies that they were back to being a problem.

Due to Malta's strategic location, the island served as a great gateway between the western and eastern parts of the Mediterranean. And since the Hospitallers were in firm control of it, they clashed with the Muslim corsairs and the Ottomans, who tried to consolidate their power in North Africa. The constant confrontations with the Ottomans annoyed Sultan Suleyman the Magnificent and his naval commander Dragut Reis, an infamous Muslim corsair dubbed the "uncrowned king of the Mediterranean." During the 1540s and the 1550s, a sort of rivalry emerged between the Hospitallers and Dragut. The brothers would not give the corsair the breathing room necessary to continue pirating the high seas. The latter even managed to lay siege and take the Hospitaller fortress on the island of Gozo with ten thousand corsairs in 1551, capturing the whole population of the town and sacking the order's outpost. Since the order was unable to defend itself from this raid, the Hospitallers, under the guidance of Grand Master Juan de Homedes, proceeded to build several new fortifications on the island. They also further fortified Birgu and constructed the forts of Saint Elmo and Saint Michael, both of which still dazzle visitors today.

After about a decade of back-and-forth, during which the Hospitallers resumed raiding the Muslim coast and interrupting the flow of Ottoman ships in the Mediterranean, Sultan Suleyman had had enough. In 1564, he gave Dragut the command of forty thousand or so troops with the objective of finishing what he had started about forty years earlier at Rhodes. The word of the approaching Ottoman fleet soon reached Malta, and Grand Master Jean Parisot de Valette hurried to organize a sound defense. As the brothers were putting up defenses around the island, he asked for help from overseas but was only sent about four hundred Spanish men, although different counts promised the order their help.

In May 1565, the Ottomans started landing at Malta, a move that grabbed Europe's attention. An Ottoman triumph at Malta would have meant the Turks would possess a sound base of operations from which they could plan an invasion of Italy and further expand their borders. The Hospitallers garrisoning the fortifications were vastly outnumbered by their foe, but time was on their side. The Ottomans were far from their home, which meant they could not extend their siege for too long, especially since the order's trusted friends, Don Garcia de Toledo and Melchor de Robles, were mustering up their own armies to help the Hospitallers.

The Turks' first target was Fort Saint Elmo, which had been specifically built to withstand an attack from the sea. It was strategically placed on the tip of a ridge thrust inward into the sea. Taking the fort was necessary if the Turkish ships wished to advance closer to the port of Birgu, where the main Hospitaller defense was organized. Dragut personally assumed the command of the siege in late May and made sure to soften its defenses with constant bombardments before ordering his men to breach the walls. The brothers answered with artillery and arrow fire of their own but were eventually overwhelmed by late June. Still, the capture of Saint Elmo cost the Ottomans about five thousand or so troops, compared to a couple of hundred Hospitallers who died defending the fort or fell prisoner. Most importantly, one of the Ottoman casualties would be commander Dragut, something that definitely came as a shock to the Turks. Nevertheless, the Ottomans were still in a favorable position with their numbers and continued their advance on other Hospitaller strongholds in a few days.

The fall of Saint Elmo was, in part, caused by the order's allies, who were unable to bring the reinforcements they had promised the grand master before the beginning of the siege. They had tried to get to the island, but the Ottoman ships, which were more numerous and mightier, dissuaded them from approaching. Eventually, de Robles made it to Malta in late June after Saint Elmo had already fallen. Although disappointed with the tardiness of the reinforcements, his troops were warmly received at Birgu by the Hospitallers under cover of night.

Mustafa Pasha took over the command of the Ottoman forces. In July, he proceeded to heavily bombard the other fortifications of the Hospitallers, including Birgu. He tried to break through the order's defenses several times but failed on all occasions, as he was driven back by a barrage of arrows that descended upon his men once they approached the mighty walls of the Hospitaller castles. At night, the Hospitallers sent small groups of soldiers outside their walls to disrupt the Ottoman camp on land, something that stalled the attackers even more.

Despite the defenders' bravery, they had been reduced to desperation. They had lost about five thousand men in action, which was the vast majority of their forces. By September, Birgu's defense comprised several hundred men at best, and with the walls slowly crumbling from the constant fire of Ottoman guns, it seemed as if the end was close. On the other hand, Mustafa Pasha failed to break through and realized that winter was approaching. He needed to produce results in the coming weeks if he did not want to anger his sultan back home.

However, even though the Ottomans hurled more and more men at the defenders, they were unable to crack the Hospitallers, who, after four months of the siege, finally received the promised reinforcements from Garcia de Toledo. He convinced the Spanish king, Philip II, to send the order a large army of about sixteen thousand men. Managing to heroically sail from Sicily during the night, evading the Ottoman sea patrols, the fleet finally arrived on September 7th, 1565. By the time the attackers realized what was going on, it was too late. The Ottomans started fleeing the battlefield, with their commander unable to inspire them to stay and continue the siege. They got on their ships and sailed back to Constantinople without looking back. The Great Siege of Malta was over. The Knights Hospitaller stood victorious.

Conclusion

The Great Siege of Malta remains one of the most influential and iconic battles of the Late Middle Ages. It was not only Suleyman the Magnificent's greatest defeat but also undoubtedly the Hospitallers' finest victory, proving once again the might of the warrior monks about five hundred years after the creation of the hospital in Jerusalem. The Hospitallers distinguished themselves with their skill and bravery, as they had done countless times in the past. And the Christian victory in Malta had a huge strategic impact on Europe's struggles against the Ottoman Empire, which was at the height of its power. No one knows what would have happened if the Ottoman soldiers had managed to take Malta—the naval gateway between the eastern and western parts of the Mediterranean.

The Great Siege of Malta marks the final significant military action in which the Hospitallers were involved, although, of course, the order continued its military activities for many centuries after the siege. For the next hundred years, the Hospitallers rebuilt their island from almost total ruin and refortified Malta, making it one of the most well-defended places in medieval Europe. For quite a while, the order was under the jurisdiction of the Sicilian Viceroyalty. A steady flow of donations and booty from raiding hostile Muslim ships catapulted the Hospitallers close to the height of their power. The transformation of Malta from a barren island into a defensive powerhouse is a testament to the order's prosperity following the victory at the siege. The Hospitallers also had some possessions in the New World. They bought several Caribbean islands from France in the mid-17th century, which they held for over a decade.

But while these endeavors kept the Hospitallers' hands full for over a century and a half, and despite the relative safety they had achieved on their island, the Knights Hospitaller would slowly enter a period of steady decline beginning in the latter half of the 17th century. In truth, by that time, the military orders were largely out of fashion. Even the Teutonic Order, which held a considerable number of territories along the Baltic coast, was eventually reduced to pieces by rival Christian nations. The crusading spirit, which had helped the Hospitallers prosper from the 11th to the 13th century, was long gone, which means the European nations had no need for the Knights Hospitaller. Soon enough, due to the relative decline of the Ottomans and the technological and intellectual advancements of the West, the Europeans emerged as dominant forces in the region, taking back control of the Mediterranean and becoming masters of most of the world.

Still, the Knights Hospitaller continued its humble existence, having built up great structures on Malta, most of which are still largely intact today. Due to the decline in the number of recruits and funds, the great European nations came to fully disregard the order in their political processes, although they still recognized its symbolic importance. Eventually, Napoleon seized Malta and the Hospitaller possessions on it, causing the order to go bankrupt in the early 1800s and pushing it to the brink of extinction. Still, the tradition was maintained by the surviving brothers during the French and subsequent English occupation until Malta finally got its independence in 1964, emerging as a sovereign nation.

Realizing their importance, the Hospitallers decided to put away their swords and instead pursue humanitarian activities throughout Europe, going back to their humble roots as caretakers of the needy at St. John's Hospital in Jerusalem. The order was officially renamed in the 19th century to "Sovereign Military Hospitaller Order of St. John of Jerusalem, of Rhodes, and of Malta," and their new headquarters were organized in Rome in the 1800s in the Palazzo Malta, which they had owned since 1630. The Italian government has officially recognized the place as an extraterritorial enclave in its territory, and the order still continues to operate today after nearly a millennium since its founding.

All in all, the Knights Hospitaller remains one of the most iconic parts of the history of Christianity, with its humble origins, high highs, and low lows. The military order has accumulated a great legacy throughout the many centuries of its existence, including the magnificent castles all throughout Europe and the Levant that still stand today. The Hospitallers were not only devout Christians and brave warriors. They were, above all, passionate caretakers of the needy and never lost track of their original purpose. Today, they are deservedly associated with knighthood, chivalry, sacrifice, and discipline, and they continue to adapt to the changing times.

Here's another book by Captivating History that you might like

THE CRUSADES

A CAPTIVATING GUIDE TO THE MILITARY EXPEDITIONS DURING THE MIDDLE AGES THAT DEPARTED FROM EUROPE WITH THE GOAL TO FREE JERUSALEM AND AID CHRISTIANITY IN THE HOLY LAND

CAPTIVATING HISTORY

Free Bonus from Captivating History (Available for a Limited time)

Hi History Lovers!

Now you have a chance to join our exclusive history list so you can get your first history ebook for free as well as discounts and a potential to get more history books for free! Simply visit the link below to join.

Captivatinghistory.com/ebook

Also, make sure to follow us on Facebook, Twitter and Youtube by searching for Captivating History.

Sources

Britannica, T. Editors of Encyclopedia (2022, December 23). Hospitallers. Encyclopedia Britannica. https://www.britannica.com/topic/Hospitallers.

Brodman, J. W. (2001). "Rule and Identity: The Case of the Military Orders." The Catholic Historical Review, 87(3), 383-400. http://www.jstor.org/stable/25025970.

Carr, J. (2016). The Knights Hospitaller: A Military History of the Knights of St John. Casemate Publishers.

Castillo, D. (1993). "'The Knights Cannot Be Admitted': Maltese Nationalism, the Knights of St. John, and the French Occupation of 1798-1800." The Catholic Historical Review, 79(3), 434-453. http://www.jstor.org/stable/25024071.

Helen Vella Bonavita. (2002). "Key to Christendom: The 1565 Siege of Malta, Its Histories, and Their Use in Reformation Polemic." The Sixteenth Century Journal, 33(4), 1021-1043. https://doi.org/10.2307/4144120.

Luttrell, A. T. (1958). "Venice and the Knights Hospitallers of Rhodes in the Fourteenth Century." Papers of the British School at Rome, 26, 195-212.

Nicholson, H. J. (2001). The Knights Hospitaller. Boydell & Brewer.

Powell, J. M. (2007). "Church and Crusade: Frederick II and Louis IX." The Catholic Historical Review, 93(2), vi-264. http://www.jstor.org/stable/25166835.

Riley-Smith, J. (2012). The Knights Hospitaller in the Levant, c. 1070-1309. Springer.

Riley-Smith, J. S. C., & Riley-Smith, J. (2003). The First Crusade and Idea of Crusading. A&C Black.

Printed in Great Britain
by Amazon